To Sing Once More

To Sing Once More

Sorrow, Joy, and the Dog I Loved

LAMBERT ZUIDERVAART

RESOURCE *Publications* · Eugene, Oregon

TO SING ONCE MORE
Sorrow, Joy, and the Dog I Loved

Copyright © 2021 Lambert Zuidervaart. All rights reserved. Except for brief quotations in critical publications or reviews, no part of this book may be reproduced in any manner without prior written permission from the publisher. Write: Permissions, Wipf and Stock Publishers, 199 W. 8th Ave., Suite 3, Eugene, OR 97401.

The publisher has given permission to use quotations from the following copyrighted lyrics.

"Never-Ending Road (Amhrán Duit)" and "Penelope's Song"
By Loreena McKennitt
Published by Quinlan Road Music Ltd
Any reference to Loreena McKennitt in this book does not imply the artist's approval or endorsement of the work.

Resource Publications
An Imprint of Wipf and Stock Publishers
199 W. 8th Ave., Suite 3
Eugene, OR 97401

www.wipfandstock.com

PAPERBACK ISBN: 978-1-7252-8568-2
HARDCOVER ISBN: 978-1-7252-8567-5
EBOOK ISBN: 978-1-7252-8569-9

01/19/21

For Mervin and to the memory of Mom and Dad Recker

Contents

Preface		ix
1	Release	1
2	Dreamcatcher	5
3	Little Star	9
4	Training	13
5	The Call	17
6	Circle Dance	21
7	Sunset	25
8	Dusk	30
9	Deep Midnight	33
10	Zigzag	38
11	Cradle Song	43
12	Nightmare	47
13	Farewell	52
14	Journey's End	57
15	Spirit Traces	61
Epilogue: Dear Hannah		63
Acknowledgments		65
Endnotes		67

Preface

I felt an urge to write about Hannah Estelle, our beautiful and affectionate Golden Retriever, long before she died due to bone cancer in December 2018. When I finally began to write, a half year after Hannah's death, I sensed keenly her role in my life as a musician. At a time of deep sadness, her puppy presence helped me learn to sing again; during the cancer-wracked months that ended her life, my singing to Hannah helped her leave. The chapters in this memoir give voice to these interwoven lines. They are dog songs: lyrical reflections on a dear dog's life that express gratitude for how she inspired me to sing.

The phrase "dog songs" comes from the title of a book of poetry by the late Mary Oliver. Her book celebrates the special bonds between humans and their dogs. Although the chapters that follow do not pretend to match the brevity and wit of Oliver's poems, I hope to have echoed some of her admiration and thankfulness for how dog friends touch human lives.

The song that begins my last chapter comes from another American poet, James Agee. Well-known among vocalists, his poem "Sure on This Shining Night" has been set to music by Samuel Barber and Morten Lauridsen, both of them masters of the lyrical phrase. Agee's poem captures in astonishingly few lines the complex overtones of healing and loss that resound through the story I tell of Hannah Estelle; it casts light and shadows on the entire book.

I could say something similar about song texts that lead into other chapters. Although from different centuries and in diverse musical settings and genres, all of them give voice to my experience

Preface

during Hannah's life. Some I sang, whether as a soloist or as a member of vocal ensembles. Others I listened to at crucial moments. And still others, especially the songs by Johannes Brahms and Loreena McKennitt, I both heard and sang, repeatedly, as Hannah's life neared its end.

The Latin proverb on the keyboard instrument in *The Music Lesson*, a well-known painting by Johannes Vermeer, reminds us: *Music is the companion of joy, a balm for sorrow.* That is how I've experienced the songs whose texts I quote. I hope my dog songs speak to your own joys and sorrows.

LAMBERT ZUIDERVAART
Grand Rapids, Michigan

1

Release

> The people that walked in darkness have seen a great light:
> and they that dwell in the land of the shadow of death,
> upon them hath the light shined.
>
> —Händel's *Messiah*[1]

Puppy Hannah joined our household during a time of loss. Our goddaughter Esther Hart had died of colon cancer in early April 2007. She was like both a daughter and a sister to my wife, Joyce. As we mourned Esther's death, I also continued to grieve the loss of Rosa, our Golden Labrador, more than two years earlier. When I finished drafting a memoir to honor Rosa in May 2007,[2] my grief felt just as jagged as on the day she died.

Yet it was also a time of healing. In late June, due to unexplained ailments, I began to see a naturopath. At the end of our first consultation she gave me a homeopathic pill—to help release my grief, I later learned. The next week, responding to a pent-up desire to sing, I attended the Beach Summer Voice Program, a four-day vocal workshop held at Bellefair United Church in Toronto's east end. Although trained as an instrumentalist and experienced as a choral singer, I had never taken individual voice lessons. The workshop would provide these and prepare me to solo in a public recital when the workshop ended.

The workshop also offered training in the Alexander Technique. The technique teaches vocalists how to refocus their movement and posture, letting energy flow freely from the lower spine and up and out. On the second afternoon of the workshop, I learned to walk while maintaining the right posture. I felt as if floating above the floor—quite unlike my hunched-over heaviness that morning, when I had reread and edited my memoir for Rosa.

Right after this airy stroll, I had a voice lesson with Marjorie, the director of the workshop. We began with warm-up exercises. Then she asked which piece I wanted to work on. "I'd love to try the bass aria 'The People That Walked in Darkness' from Händel's *Messiah*," I replied. I sang a page or so. Marjorie stopped me to help me breathe properly for the long melismatic phrases. I started again.

"Now try to recapture the feeling you had a few minutes ago when you walked using the Alexander Technique," she said. "Imagine that you are drawing your breath directly from the ground beneath your feet. Let it flow through your legs to your torso and up and out."

"I'll try," I said.

I paused to collect myself and visualize. I began again. Suddenly my voice opened up, in a releasement I'd never felt before. Then, as I headed through the second phrase and came to "have seen a great light," a tsunami of sorrow crashed through my body, smashing every carefully constructed constraint. I began to cry, unreservedly, sob after sob rolling out as if they'd never end.

Marjorie was cool. "That's OK," she reassured. "Just take your time; this often happens when singers connect with something deep inside." After regaining my composure, I resumed where I'd left off and sang the solo through to the end, on the verge of melting down several times, but with a rich vocal quality I didn't know I had. In a wholly unexpected way, I'd been singing, yes, really singing, a song of loss and healing.

When I met with my naturopath the next morning, I told her what had happened. Unsurprised, she affirmed it as a breakthrough. But only several sessions later did she say what she had given me before the workshop and what it was for. Already then she had diagnosed unresolved sorrow as the core of my health problems. And her final remedy, beyond a grief-releasing homeopathic pill, was just as unexpected as the vocal meltdown her tablet helped trigger. During my last July session, she proclaimed: "Lambert, the single most important step you can take along the path of healing is to adopt a puppy—not a dog, but a puppy."

That was just what I needed to hear. I'd been putting this step off, telling myself how difficult it would be to find a suitable successor to Rosa, hesitating about the effort required to look, and worrying about the time and expenses a new dog would involve. Immediately I went online to locate a suitable breeder. I found one called Cooperslane Kennel. One phone call and an email later I had an appointment to see their dogs the next day.

Although nearly instantaneous, the decision was not easy. Scenes of danger, loss, and recovery troubled my dreams that night:

> Scene 1: Although I am late to attend a performance of Händel's *Messiah*, I find a comfortable seat with an unobstructed view. But then others arrive. In the confusion that follows, I lose my seat.

> Scene 2: By surprise, a dog shows up who looks a lot like Rosa did in her youth. The new dog and I bond right away; she always wants to be near me. Sometimes I panic and think she has strayed off. But when I call her, she quickly reappears. The last time she returns, however, she looks different. In her head and shoulders, she resembles a Labradoodle rather than a Golden Lab.

> Scene 3: I am out hiking with my friend Ron when I look up and see two airplanes. One is a commercial airliner, the other a military transport plane. Fire and smoke surround the military plane. Instantly I run for cover and urge Ron to do the same. I dart into a wooded area as debris begins to hit all around. I sit next to a tree, covering my head. Yet I know this won't protect me from the larger chunks. So I run again, down an embankment to another tree. This tree is crooked enough to let me sit under its trunk. I survive.

In these troubled dream scenes, I lose my place, I temporarily lose a new canine companion, and I lose a sense of safety. My new openness to adopting a puppy carried all of those anxieties with it. Would my life be so disrupted that I could no longer stay focused, losing my seat at the performance? Would the dog I adopt live up to my exaggerated expectations for Rosa's successor? Would all hell break loose once I stopped worrying about making a decision to adopt and, as it were, just took a hike? Yet a still small voice of encouragement also sounds in the last two scenes. For the new dog and I bond quickly and deeply, and she comes right away when I call. And, despite the devastation raining down on my hike, I find a place where I can survive. Thus I tried to reassure myself in my dreams that the path my naturopath prescribed could indeed lead to healing.

So on Sunday morning, July 22, 2007, Joyce and I drove out to Cooperslane Kennel, in the countryside northwest of Toronto near the village of Arthur, Ontario, to meet Valerie Cooper and her husband, Brian. They showed us all their adult dogs, both Labrador Retrievers and Golden Retrievers, and they let us hold some puppies from a Lab litter. Their Golden Retriever litter was too young to be seen by customers. But we did meet Mary, the lovely first-time mother of twelve Golden puppies born on July 7, the day after I had soloed through my sorrow. Mary's gentle beauty breathed away my hesitations and worries. We asked Valerie to reserve a female puppy from Mary's litter.

On my walk that evening, I talked with Rosa, who still accompanied me in spirit. I told her that we planned to adopt a puppy she would like. The puppy would not replace her in our hearts, I said, but would bring us the same joy Rosa offered. I felt happy. And I felt Rosa was happy too: her companion who walked in darkness had seen a great light.

2

Dreamcatcher

> Here is my heart and I give it to you
> Take me with you across this land
> These are my dreams, so simple, so few
> Dreams we hold in the palm of our hands
>
> —Loreena McKennitt[3]

I MIGHT HAVE HELD Hannah for the first time on August 2, 2007. Joyce and I had been in Stratford, Ontario, to celebrate my fifty-seventh birthday at the Stratford Festival. Driving back to our home in Toronto, we stopped at Cooperslane Kennel to visit Mary's four-week-old puppies, twelve cuddlable dumplings of golden fur, each one eager to greet us. Valerie, who would decide later which puppy was ours, let us hold several. One puppy fell fast asleep in my arms. I'll never know for sure, but I like to think it was Hannah. In later years she'd be just as calm and just as connected to me as this little dozing dog.

The days leading up to our visit were anything but calm. The day before, on my birthday, I learned that my ninety-three-year-old mother had suffered a stroke; she never fully recovered. A few days before that, Joyce and I had attended the ceremonial scattering of Esther Hart's ashes on Georgian Bay. The event took place not far from Ontario's Awenda Provincial Park, where I had often camped with Rosa, and near where the Hart family cottage had once stood. As Esther's father, brother, and partner waded out with her ashes, Joyce and I stood with others on the shoreline. We watched and waited for a goddaughter who would never return. Yet we knew that Sophie, Esther's little three-and-a-half-year-old daughter, whom Joyce had cared for during Esther's three-year illness, would always be our goddaughter too.

These experiences shaped our search for the right name to give the puppy who would join our household at the end of August. During our stay at Awenda and then in Stratford, Joyce and I brainstormed through a long list of names. Eventually we chose two and decided to give our puppy a double name: Hannah Estelle. Because she came from distinguished lines of purebred Golden Retrievers, her official name would be Cooperslane Hannah Estelle. But we would simply call her Hannah, using the soft "ah" vowels of the German pronunciation ("HAH-nah").

The name Hannah means "grace" or, more elaborately, "God has graced us with a child." It can also mean "beauty" or "passionate." The meaning "grace" derives from the story of Hannah in the first book of Samuel. Hannah was married to Elkanah, who had a second wife named Peninnah. Peninnah bore many children. Hannah, to her great sorrow, had none. When Eli the priest observed Hannah praying silently yet fervently for a child, he told her not to make "a drunken spectacle" of herself (1 Sam 1:14, NRSV). But after she explained her entranced vexation, he offered his blessing. Not long afterward Hannah gave birth to a son. She named him Samuel and dedicated him to the priesthood. Then follows the Song of Hannah (1 Sam 2:1–10), which resembles the Magnificat of Mary, the mother of Jesus (Luke 1:46–55). The song gives thanks for the favor Hannah found when God graced her with a child.[4]

This story resonates in the significance the name Hannah has for Joyce and me. Our goddaughter Esther gave birth to Sophie at a relatively late age and did not live to see her only child grow up. Yet, at a still later age, we, who have no children of our own, have been graced with Sophie, the beautiful and passionate child of our goddaughter. We hold Esther's dreams for Sophie in our own hearts.

Estelle, our puppy's second name, also has personal significance. It means "star," reminding us of our Esther, whose name also means "star." Estelle also became the name of the toy dog that Hannah slept with every night until the day she died. Hannah Estelle would remind us of Esther and her dreams; the puppy would be our gracious star.

Does that seem like too much weight to put on naming a puppy? Perhaps. Yet adopting Hannah was a weighty decision. Until recently I had not thought I could adopt another dog. The burden of grief felt too great. Now, almost miraculously, I was welcoming a puppy—not a dog, but a puppy—whom I had not officially met. And in welcoming her I laid myself open for both the joys and the sorrows she would bring, open for dreams to be held in the palm of our hands.

Late one evening, the day before we brought our new puppy home, I wrote her this letter of welcome:

> Dear Hannah,
>
> Joyce and I are eager to meet you and welcome you into our home. We may have held you a few weeks ago—we do not know for sure, because Valerie had not decided then which of your mother's puppies would be ours.
>
> I hope you like your name: Hannah Estelle. It expresses our hope for you and for Sophie and for ourselves: God's gracious star. You will like Sophie. She is a precious child who lost her mother, our goddaughter Esther, to cancer this year. Your second name reminds us of Esther, our bright morning star.
>
> More than two and a half years ago our Rosa died. She was a beautiful and loving companion. I miss her still. Just today I retraced my last walk with her on February 21, 2005. You will use Rosa's water and food dishes, her leash, and some of her toys. But now they are yours, as we are too.
>
> So we welcome you into our home. May we be as gentle and loving as Rosa taught us to be. And may you grace our lives with your unique friendship well into our senior years.

Love,
Lambert

    The letter, I now see, is more than a welcome. It is also a promise and a prayer. It is a promise of love and a prayer for healing. Just a few days earlier I had heard Loreena McKennitt's song "Never-Ending Road" for the first time. Her lyrics capture my promise and prayer for Hannah Estelle, the precious puppy I would soon meet: "Here is my heart and I give it to you / Take me with you across this land." The next day Joyce and I would hold Hannah, our dream dog, in the palm of our hands. Our shared journey would begin.

3
Little Star

> As your bright and tiny spark
> Lights the traveler in the dark,
> Though I know not what you are,
> Twinkle, twinkle, little star.
>
> —Jane Taylor[5]

At last Hannah's adoption day arrived: August 31, 2007, the day before she would turn eight weeks old. Our house was ready: dog crate assembled in our second-floor bedroom, dishes and toys arranged on the first floor, slippers and other chewable distractions removed. As recommended by Valerie Cooper, the breeder, we had bought a stuffed toy animal for Hannah. It was a fluffy beige dog, about Hannah's adoptive size, that we named Estelle. We brought Estelle along so Valerie could rub it on Hannah's mother and littermates. Estelle would keep their comforting smells close when Hannah left her dog family.

It took us nearly two hours to drive to Cooperslane Kennel from our home in Toronto's east end. We arrived just before noon on a sunny late summer morning. After talking with Valerie in her house and completing the paperwork, we walked out to the kennel. There Valerie rubbed Estelle on Hannah's family; we returned to the house carrying both Estelle and our sweet and gentle puppy.

Then Valerie placed Hannah on a towel at table height and showed us how to brush her and clean her ears—important hygiene for a puppy who would become an active water dog with sensitive ears and a luxurious coat. Even then we could see the faintly darker hairlines, running like mascara toward Hannah's ears, that gave her what we later called Cleopatra eyes.

We carried Hannah and Estelle out to the car to begin our journey home. At first Joyce drove and I held our puppy on my lap. But Hannah was not used to car rides. Nor was she ready to leave her family. She whined and cried her distress. About halfway to Toronto we switched roles: I would drive, and Joyce would hold Hannah. Soon Hannah fell asleep in Joyce's arms, like the tiny puppy I had held earlier that month.

An hour after we arrived home, Hannah and I sat outside together for the first time, on the front porch. As she played with her stuffed dog and dozed beside it, I reviewed notes on puppy training and took photos of her. Later, when I brought Hannah upstairs to her kennel, she was eager to go in and greet Estelle, whom she treated like a littermate. Soon she settled in her kennel, and I left the bedroom to do office work in the adjoining room.

That night Hannah slept straight through without a peep. She got up when I awoke and seemed eager to be with me. After she did her morning business and ate breakfast, we trained on "come," a dog's first commandment—or request, as one soulful dog book put it. She learned it just like that. When I went upstairs to my home office to catch up on email, she curled up right at my feet to sleep. A few hours later, after I had carried her a couple of blocks to buy the Saturday newspaper, she again slept nearby as I read on the front porch. Our lifelong companionship would often find us relaxing together outdoors. Although Hannah never lounged on indoor furniture (following another of our "requests"), she always headed for outdoor benches, logs, and picnic tables—any raised surface where she could sit near me and survey the world and, of course, receive my petting and praise.

The day before, a few hours after we returned from Cooperslane Kennel, Hannah met little Sophie, our other family member. Not quite four years old, Sophie quickly bonded with Hannah. First

Hannah followed her around in our backyard. Next Joyce showed Sophie how to talk to Hannah. Then, when Joyce and Sophie crouched down to pet her, Hannah made the submissive gesture that always endeared her to friends and strangers alike, even in her last year of life: she rolled over on her back, tender tummy exposed, and grinned an invitation to give her a belly rub. Hannah would show special affection for children in the years ahead.

Yet not all interactions between Sophie and Hannah exuded sweetness and light. A few months later, when Hannah had already tripled in size, I took a trip to visit my hospitalized mother in north central California and attend a philosophy conference in Los Angeles. I was away for a week. That left Joyce in charge of two youngsters, one an energetic four-month-old puppy and the other a precocious nearly four-year-old preschooler.

Every weekday Joyce would meet Sophie at her French-language preschool and bring her to our house until David, Sophie's dad, picked her up on his way home from work. One weekday afternoon midway through my stay in California, Sophie returned from preschool wearing her favorite socks. They were decorated with the Japanese cartoon character called Hello Kitty. Sophie's feet were warm. So she decided to take off her special socks. Joyce put them on the kitchen window ledge, safely out of Hannah's reach.

A little later, when Sophie wanted to put her socks back on, Joyce could find only one. They looked all around, but the other sock had gone missing. Slowly it dawned on Joyce: perhaps the other sock fell, to be snatched up by our voracious canine vacuum cleaner. Once Joyce thought this, she knew it was so. Quickly bundling both youngsters into the back seat of the car, she rushed to Woodbine Animal Clinic, with Sophie wailing, "Why did Hannah eat my Hello Kitty sock?"

Joyce had to leave Hannah at the clinic for induced vomiting and observation. When she called later about picking Hannah up, the receptionist asked whether Joyce wanted what they had forcibly retrieved from our Golden Retriever. Sophie definitely wanted her special sock back. She simply could not fathom Hannah's theft. But Joyce had praised Sophie for being patient with Hannah, and that lessened Sophie's distress. When Joyce and Sophie returned from the clinic the second time, they brought home, along with Hannah, a neatly ziplocked, very smelly, but otherwise undamaged Hello Kitty sock. Looking at the back seat through the rearview mirror, Joyce saw Sophie lean over to our hoovering hound and proudly proclaim: "I was very patient with you, Hannah." The mystery of Hannah's misbehavior might not have been solved, but Sophie had set the terms for their future together.

And so began our journey with Hannah Estelle, a gorgeous Golden Retriever with twinkling Cleopatra eyes. She always slept near us, cuddling with her littermate, Estelle, and she always had a soft spot for children, including their clothes. Her calmness alongside me, both indoors and out, made even more astonishing her athleticism and mischief. Through it all she lived up to the meaning of her name: gracious star. Although, like Sophie, I never fully understood Hannah's absolute fetish for socks, mittens, and gloves, she became the bright and tiny spark lighting a traveler who'd walked in the dark.

4

Training

> If I should die and leave you here awhile
> Be not like others, sore undone
> who keep long vigils by the silent dust and weep.
> For my sake return to life and smile
> nerving thy heart and trembling hands
> to do something to comfort other hearts than thine.
> Complete those dear unfinished tasks of mine,
> And I, perchance, may therein comfort you.
>
> —MARY LEE HALL[6]

PATIENCE, SAYS THE PROVERB, is a virtue. Hannah's unexpected escapades made me more virtuous. Often her most disruptive antics happened at the worst times. One took place when she was six months old.

January 19, 2008, a Saturday, would have been our goddaughter Esther Hart's fortieth birthday. She had died on April 3 the previous year. To remember Esther on her birthday, Joyce and I, together with Esther's parents, Henk and Anita Hart, had organized a public memorial recital at 2:00 that afternoon. It would take place at Toronto's Institute for Christian Studies (ICS), the graduate school for interdisciplinary philosophy where Henk had taught and where I was his successor. Henk and Anita had decided to donate Esther's piano to ICS; the recital would dedicate the piano in Esther's memory. Her parents would speak, Joyce and I would play piano duets, a fellow professor and an ICS supporter would play piano solos, and two soprano soloists would sing. We called the program "Prayers and Lullabies: Songs to Dedicate the Esther Hart Memorial Piano."

I had also arranged for a quartet to sing "Cantique de Jean Racine" by Gabriel Fauré, a well-known prayer in the nineteenth-century French vocal repertoire. Joyce, who had given Esther her first piano lessons, would accompany us. The quartet came from the Beach United Church choir, which I had joined two years earlier. I was to sing the bass part, our conductor Mervin Fick the tenor, and our fellow choristers Karen Johnston and Karen Watson would be the alto and soprano. This would be the first time we had performed as a quartet. It would also be my first attempt at soloistic singing since the summer vocal workshop where I had melted down. To prepare for an intense experience, our quartet had scheduled a final rehearsal at ICS that morning. Joyce and I planned to leave the house at 10:30 AM.

But first I needed to give Hannah her morning constitutional and playtime before a long day without us. Joyce and I did not expect to return home until 6:00 PM. We had asked Steve, our next-door neighbor, to look in on Hannah while we were away. Feeling pressured, I quickly walked her the five or so blocks to Cassels Park.

It was a brisk and sunny winter morning. The recent snow had melted and piles of autumn leaves, which the city had failed to remove, punctuated the parkland. The dogs loved to tear around these piles. But Hannah did not simply dash past them. Her supersensitive nose also tracked a hidden treasure. Romping with another dog, Hannah suddenly veered off into one of the leaf piles. Before I knew what was happening, she swung a trophy out of the leaves, flinging it into the air and prancing like a pony. Remembering the fate of Sophie's sock, I yelled, "Hannah, come. Hannah, drop it!" No way! Still flinging and prancing, she would not come closer. Another dog owner, trying to help, also called. Hannah approached her and sat at the helpful woman's feet, expecting a treat. When the woman bent down to remove the prize, Hannah promptly swallowed it. I immediately grabbed and leashed her and marched her out of the park.

Just that quickly we faced another canine crisis, on a day already fraught with intense emotion. It was 9:45 AM when Hannah and I arrived home. I had just enough time to call the animal clinic, bring Hannah in, and leave her there. Then I rushed home to change clothes so Joyce and I could get to our rehearsal. As I changed, Joyce called Steve to let him know the latest. He offered to pick Hannah up from the animal clinic and bring her home before it closed for the rest of the weekend. But we still did not know what she had swallowed. As we left for our rehearsal, we worried.

Later, calling Steve before the recital began, we found out Hannah was home and healthy. Upon receiving a double injection to induce vomiting she had upchucked the dirty leather cover of a lost baseball, all in one piece. That's what had given her such joy—and, of course, the discomfort that followed. An experienced dog owner, Steve assured me that dogs with a garbage fetish eventually figure out what not to swallow. Hannah was very smart. Naively I hoped she would learn from two unpleasant experiences in less than three months, first with the Hello Kitty sock and now with the baseball leather. But it would be seven eventful years before she stopped scarfing down cast-off cloth.

Despite Hannah's adolescent antics, the recital that day sealed my decision to take individual voice lessons. Nothing compares with singing a passionate prayer of renewal for those who are grieving a deep loss, as our quartet had done. Lending my voice to song, I now felt, could help comfort others and not only me.

It could also help complete one of Esther's unfinished tasks. Esther had a lovely light soprano voice. She had studied with the Canadian vocalist Denise Williams, who also sang at the memorial recital. When Joyce and I moved to Toronto in 2002 Esther and I had talked about joining a choir together. That never happened. Yet now, at an event in her memory, I had finally sung on her behalf. I wanted to continue.

Yet to sing well, I realized, I needed to be taught. Although I'd learned by then that I loved to sing, I had not learned to sing in a way that I loved. Just as Hannah, to become a discriminating retriever, required more training, so to become an accomplished singer I needed vocal instruction. Two and a half weeks later I had my first voice lesson with Mervin Fick. For the next four years, until Joyce and I moved to Grand Rapids, Mervin gave me weekly hour-long lessons as our schedules permitted. From these lessons many opportunities emerged for solo, small ensemble, and choral singing, including the Toronto Beach Chorale, which I helped co-found later in 2008.

Most of the voice lessons happened at the piano on the first floor in our house. Hannah made sure she was included. As Mervin taught me and accompanied my singing, she would lie under the baby grand piano, her head directly on his feet and often blocking the pedals. Occasionally he would need to stop playing and nudge her head away. Then, when my voice had really warmed up and more complex overtones began to ring out, Hannah would retreat to the next room. Sometimes she headed all the way up to the second floor. I took her temporary departures as compliments rather than criticisms: the increasingly rich timbre of my voice had become too much for her to bear! Yet Hannah, who always greeted Mervin at the front door when he arrived, regularly showed up again to say goodbye when the lesson ended.

During the memorial recital on Esther's fortieth birthday, our friend Karen Watson sang the poignant solo "Turn Again to Life." The song urges us not to lose ourselves in grief at a loved one's death. Instead, for her sake, we should comfort others. And in our completing her "dear unfinished tasks," she might comfort us. Whether learning from Mervin how to sing better or gaining from Hannah the patience needed to train her, I discovered, as the song says, how to "return to life and smile." And if once in a while, like Hannah at my voice lessons, I needed to retreat, that too could help me return to comfort other hearts than mine.

5
The Call

Hannah and I celebrated her first three birthdays at Ontario's Awenda Provincial Park. Although we camped elsewhere in later years and not always on her birthday, once each summer and sometimes twice I would load up the car with camping gear, put Hannah in the back, and drive a few hours to one of our favorite parks. To be a favorite, a park needed to offer spacious campgrounds, ample forests, dog-friendly beaches, and many miles of hiking trails. Mosquitoes never annoyed Hannah, though they often bothered me. Thunderstorms, however, made her frantic, whereas I welcomed the challenges of camping in the rain. So she and I learned to compromise about when to camp. Increasingly, as we both aged, I timed our trips around predictions for three sunny days without mosquitoes.

Our first trip, for Hannah's first birthday, ignored these not-yet-settled rules for happy campers. The weather was hot and muggy. Rain started soon after we arrived and before I could finish putting up our tent. Thunderstorms rumbled in from Georgian Bay both day and night. To this, hordes of mosquitoes added their misery. Yet Hannah was mostly curious rather than perturbed. Each new event added to her adventure: unloading the car, fixing supper over a camp stove, building a campfire, walking along the Dunes Trail in the dark, sleeping amid constant night sounds in a thin-walled tent, awaking to trilling birdsongs after a driving rain. The first evening, if she had not been on a staked chain, she would have walked right into the fire pit to seize a burning stick. She showed more caution, however, during our after-dusk hike: Hannah heard and smelled animals that I could not see. And when a thunderstorm struck after midnight, she abandoned her dog blanket and wedged herself securely between my head and the tent wall, where I could easily reach up and comfort her.

The next two days we hiked all the trails at Awenda. Hannah also swam at the dog beach where I had first sketched the memoir *Dog-Kissed Tears* in honor of Rosa. Hannah did not know why I needed to return there. Nor did she know how unsettled I felt as we walked these trails. I could not stop thinking about Rosa, even as I began new adventures with Hannah. It was as if I could not shake the past to live in the present. This split-screen experience would continue for a few more years, until Hannah and I began to frequent parks where Rosa and I had never camped. But for Hannah all of it was a new adventure. The few times I took her leash off during our extended hikes she tore around like a filly let out to pasture, running wide circles around me at breakneck speed and, when I called her back, recklessly skidding to a halt, nearly knocking me over.

By the third and final morning Hannah was an experienced camper and restless to begin the adventures of a new day. As I prepared my breakfast, she attacked a four-foot stick as if it were her stuffed dog, Estelle, frolicking back and forth to the end of her chain. So it surprised her when I started to pack up the food and supplies. She became puzzled when the tent came down and disappeared into the car. After I had packed all our gear, I turned to get Hannah. She was not in any of the expected spots. Still on her chain, she had managed to climb the picnic table, the last unexplored space in the campsite and the one where delicious odors had emanated. There she lay watching me, a front paw draped over the table's edge, as if to say: Now at last my first camping adventure is complete.

Meanwhile my own vocal adventures continued. Two weeks after the first camping trip with Hannah I attended a second four-day workshop in the Beach Summer Voice Program. There I especially worked on "The Call" from *Five Mystical Songs* by Ralph Vaughan Williams. Thanks to Mervin Fick's instruction and the new dog in my life, I was much better prepared than in the previous summer to sing with passion and without collapse.

A few weeks later I put this preparation to the test. In early August I flew to California to visit my family and attend the fortieth reunion of my high school graduating class. I especially wanted to spend time with Mom Zuidervaart, who at age ninety-four was bedridden in a skilled nursing facility. She had broken her leg a few months after her stroke in August of the previous year. Increasingly, according to my siblings who lived nearby, Mom also showed signs of dementia.

Because she shared a room with two other women, all three lying side by side, I felt self-conscious the first time my sister, Roelyn, and I visited Mom. Roelyn had told me that the woman in the next bed over did not like to be disturbed. She hated artificial light and preferred to be in the dark. But Mom instantly recognized me, and asked, "How's Joyce?" I became less self-conscious.

During my second visit, this time by myself, I told Mom I had been taking voice lessons and was singing a lot. Immediately she said, "So, sing something!" Despite the lack of privacy, realizing that I might upset Mom's roommate, and knowing my voice would carry into other rooms, I sang the first verse of "The Call":

> Come, my Way, my Truth, my Life:
> Such a Way, as gives us breath:
> Such a Truth, as ends all strife:
> Such a Life, as killeth death.[7]

Mom gazed at me as I sang, drinking the song in. When I finished, the roommate who disliked disturbances softly applauded. Then Mom asked me to sing some more. And I did, four hymns that she loved, beginning with the Doxology ("Praise God from whom all blessings flow . . . ") and, to cheer things up, concluding with the Christmas carol "Joy to the World"—admittedly an odd choice given the somber setting and the summer season in California's semi-arid Central Valley.

That became the pattern for my visits on the next two days, the last times I saw Mom alive. She would recognize me, we would talk, and when the time came to leave, I would sing. To end my last visit,

I sang three familiar songs from her favorite hymnal: "What Wondrous Love Is This," "God Be with You Till We Meet Again," and "Blest Be the Tie That Binds." Before concluding with the Doxology, I told her I would not be visiting again. She looked directly into my eyes as I sang. Then I said I loved her and hoped she would be in God's care. As I prepared to leave, Mom gave me a firm handshake and wore a gentle smile.

    Mom never recovered. But her request for my singing stayed with me, also at her funeral in June 2009. Accompanied by Roelyn, I ended my eulogy by performing in Mom's honor all three verses of Vaughan Williams' mystical song "The Call." Like Hannah on her first camping trip, I had become comfortable in new and unfamiliar circumstances. And just as my journey with Hannah had begun when a naturopath prescribed an unexpected remedy for unresolved grief—"not a dog, but a puppy"—so from then on my bedridden mother's spontaneous invitation would sustain all my vocal explorations. In singing to her about a way, a truth, and a life, I too had received The Call: "So, sing something!"

6

Circle Dance

> She comes to me when I'm feelin' down
> Inspires me without a sound
> She touches me and I get turned around
> —BILLY JOEL[8]

MY WORK LIFE DURING the four years after we adopted Hannah was stressful and intense. ICS's budget, which relied heavily on major donations, cratered during the worldwide Great Recession of 2008–2009. In response, faculty and staff had to take large salary cuts. The organization also sharply reduced rental costs by relocating from an entire floor and a half to just a half floor in the same building. So I moved my on-campus office home. During the same four years, on top of regular teaching, research, and administration, I directed three academic conferences and developed the vision for a new research center, which I then headed for two years.

 I do not think I neglected Hannah during these difficult years. I'm sure she enjoyed having me home more often now that I had no on-campus office. Yet she must have sensed my stress and tension, and she found ways to make me smile. One way was a variation on her baseball leather escapade. Our first walk each day right after breakfast often took us to Wildwood Crescent Playground and its fenced-in dog park. The park was just a few blocks from our house; many neighbors and their dogs used it. Right behind the dog park lay the tracks for passenger trains that ran past throughout the day. We called it the "Train Park." Hannah liked to catch her frisbee there and romp around with other dogs while I visited with their owners. We also met professional dog walkers who gave me tips about Hannah's health and behavior. Kim, a dog walker whom we stayed in touch with later, always called her "Hannah Banana." Hannah loved to greet her.

Unlike Kim, one of the other regulars was not friendly. An older gentleman, he lived less than a block from the park with his two large dogs, a cream-colored Golden Retriever and a black Lab. Often they showed up when Hannah and I were at the Train Park, where they walked the fenced-in perimeter, circling around and around. The older gentleman did not play with his dogs, he did not speak with other dog owners, and I never learned his name. His Golden Retriever, by contrast, was very sociable. She liked it when I talked to her and pet her. Meanwhile her owner would continue his morose stroll along the Train Park fence, his two dogs more or less following.

Hannah, however, never accepted his grumpy ways; she knew how to break his silence. Inevitably, as he walked, unused plastic poop bags would peek from the pocket of his jacket. Hannah could be in the midst of a frisbee fetch or a canine chase. If she spied a peeking poop bag, she'd dash over and deftly snatch it from Mr. Grump's pocket. Then she'd dance away, eliciting a loud, disgusted shout. He never learned to tuck the bags invisibly into his pocket, and Hannah never stopped tormenting him with playful thefts. Even though I reprimanded her and apologized for her conduct, every time I could barely suppress a smile.

Another de-stressing incident happened during our camping trip to celebrate Hannah's third birthday in July 2010. We arrived at Awenda Provincial Park in the afternoon the day before her birthday and planned to stay for three nights. Despite the swarming mosquitoes we enjoyed a relaxing trip, complete with a huge birthday beef bone that Hannah gnawed at nonstop for two hours the next afternoon. On our third afternoon Hannah enjoyed a luxurious swim at the dog beach, heading out farther and farther as I hurried to catch up and coax her back toward shore.

Just when our swimming ended rain started to fall. It let up as we hiked the three or four miles back to our campsite. But when we arrived, the rain resumed in earnest, joined by thunder and lightning. Even though I was ready to wait out the storm, Hannah refused. She made it very clear: there was no way in hell she would stay overnight amid sound and fury signifying nothing. Nor was she going to perch on the picnic table, as she had two years earlier, to watch me dismantle our campsite. No, she demanded to sit in the back of our Toyota hatchback, balefully watching as I tried to pack around her and refusing to budge from her safety zone. She had made an executive decision to end our trip a night early. On our stormy drive home, every time I recalled her lofty manner, I had to laugh.

Despite Hannah's humor, Joyce and I knew my work life would have to change. I began to apply for other academic positions and we started to talk about moving elsewhere. Nothing came of my applications. Yet eventually we did relocate, back to Grand Rapids, Michigan, where we had lived before moving to Toronto in 2002.

Meanwhile my musical avocation continued to flourish, leading to new friendships not only for Joyce and me but also for Hannah. Mervin Fick, my voice instructor, established two new vocal groups in early 2011 and asked me to join. The Esprit Chamber Chorus brought together the best singers from several of the choirs he led. We gathered once a month for an eight-hour weekend workshop and rehearsal, with the aim of recording and going on tour. Our first trip took place that summer, a three-day concert tour in Montreal, where we performed in several landmark churches: Notre-Dame Basilica, Saint Joseph Oratory, Christ Church Cathedral, and the Cathedral of Marie-Reine-du-Monde. Francine Morency, a Francophone soprano in our choir, organized the tour. She made sure we received a warm welcome at each performance.

Francine's spouse, Rudy DePaoli, was my bass partner in The Four Men, in which I sang baritone. Founded around the same time by Mervin and his fellow tenor Brian McIntosh, we were a semi-professional quartet whose concerts raised funds for the United

Church of Canada and other organizations. We sang our first concert in early February 2011 at Toronto's Trinity St. Paul's Centre to benefit Africa Files, a solidarity and justice organization. From then on we gave one or two performances a month and raised thousands of dollars for social justice causes.

In August that year Joyce and I traveled to Europe for three weeks. There I lectured at an academic conference in Amsterdam, and we vacationed in France with our friends Ron and Lucienne. Hannah needed a place to stay during this time and good people to keep her company. Francine and Rudy were the perfect hosts. Their own Golden Retriever had died about a year earlier, and they loved our Hannah. Plus, much to Hannah's delight, their backyard included both a fish pond and an outdoor swimming pool. When we took Hannah there on the evening before our trip began she promptly splashed into the pond, trying to catch the fish she could see scuttling across the bottom. Later, when Joyce and I were in Europe, Francine sent us daily chronicles, complete with photographs, of Hannah's activities: taking dips in the swimming pool, going for walks, watching the ducks at Loafer's Lake, playing fetch, and receiving frequent petting and repeated grooming from two fond caregivers.

Francine also sent me a photograph of Hannah taking my place during a Four Men rehearsal. As Brian held my sheet music in front of her and Mervin and Rudy laughed, Hannah looked on befuddled. A few months later, however, she paid them back. The Four Men held a rehearsal at our house. To achieve the best blend, we sang standing in a circle. And Hannah lay down right in the center. No matter how I coaxed her, she would not move.

Nor did we really want her to leave our circle of song. She brought joy to our making music, and our music making brought joy to her. My fellow singers must have felt, as I did, the healing quality of Hannah's humor. In the words of a song by Billy Joel our quartet often performed, I had to laugh when she revealed me. Whether dancing Train Park circles around Mr. Grump or unilaterally deciding to break up camp, Hannah had a way of approaching when I felt down, of inspiring me without a sound, of touching and turning me around. She had a way.

7

Sunset

> Now that the time has come
> Soon gone is the day
> There upon some distant shore
> You'll hear me say
> Long as the day in the summer time
> Deep as the wine-dark sea
> I'll keep your heart with mine.
> Till you come to me
>
> —Loreena McKennitt[9]

Our household moved from Toronto to Grand Rapids in mid-July 2012. Joyce and I had lived in Toronto for ten years. Hannah joined us for the last five, followed one year later by a beautiful black and white Maine Coon kitten named Measha, after the Canadian soprano Measha Brueggergosman. Once Hannah had figured out that her new housemate was neither a squeaky toy nor a stray squirrel, they became buddies. They played vigorously and often slept together on Hannah's blanket.

When we moved, Hannah and Measha received help from friends on both sides of the border, especially Susan, who adopted them for two days while the movers emptied our Toronto home, and Daryl and Dan, who sheltered all of us for several days while we waited for the moving van to arrive in Grand Rapids. But the move disrupted our pets' patterns. Afterward they no longer spent time together. Measha retreated to the third floor, where Joyce set up her new studio and office, while Hannah stayed mostly on the other two floors, close enough to greet every first-floor visitor but also to lounge in my second-floor library and office.

Hannah and I also missed the comradery at Toronto's dog parks. There had been three parks just a few blocks from our house and we had visited one or more every day. At each one Hannah had her favorite people to greet and dog friends to chase. In Grand Rapids, by contrast, until Pleasant Park opened two years later, there were no dog parks within easy walking distance of our new home in the Heritage Hill Historic District. Although Hannah never missed a chance to greet people when we strolled the neighborhood sidewalks (and to solicit a belly rub, if possible), it was not the same as running off leash with other dogs (and perhaps snatching a wool mitten or plastic bag along the way!).

Fortunately, our friend Toni had recently adopted Remy, a black and white Borador—a Border Collie / Labrador Retriever mix. Remy, who was smaller than Hannah, loved to play with her. At first they would tussle indoors. As their games became rougher, we sent them into the backyard, where they could run figure eights at full tilt. But Remy had permanently congested lungs. Soon he would declare a timeout, rushing up the steps onto our back deck and wheezing there at Hannah, who let him take a break. In a minute they would be at it again, rushing and wrestling and rolling like two crazy clowns. A few years later Mazie, a Miniature Goldendoodle puppy adopted by our friends Connie and Darlene, joined the circus. For a year or so our gatherings verged on pure mayhem, and Hannah loved it. As the older and larger dog, she knew just when to roll over or back off for the sake of her smaller playmates.

Joyce and I already had many friends and colleagues in Grand Rapids from the seventeen years we had lived there before relocating to Toronto in 2002. Now I needed to connect with the vocal music scene, which I had not belonged to before. This happened quickly when I joined the adult choir at Westminster Presbyterian Church, a thriving downtown congregation a few blocks from our house. From there new opportunities opened for solo and small ensemble singing; within a few years I would also join several other choirs.

But first I had to sort out my work life back in Toronto. I was on a half-year sabbatical when we moved to Grand Rapids. That ended in December 2012, and I planned to resume full-time work at ICS and the University of Toronto in January, driving as needed between Grand Rapids and Toronto, a six to seven-hour drive. Once I began this I quickly realized two things. First, I was ready to reduce my employment obligations. Rather than working full-time I should ask for a half-time position and teach only one semester each academic year. Second, I did not want to commute every week. It would be much better to find temporary housing in Toronto and live there with Hannah a semester at a time.

That's the arrangement I worked out until I retired at the end of June 2016. As a result, in the next few years, Hannah and I spent many days and weeks together, just the two of us. She rode back and forth to Toronto numerous times and lived with me there in small apartments with few visitors. For diversion she and I enjoyed many outings together at beaches and parks both within and outside the city.

During our weeks alone together the fondness I already had for Hannah became a heartfelt attachment. At the beginning of a work semester I would load my clothes, books, and papers into our Toyota Matrix, pack up Hannah's kennel, dishes, and toys, put her in the hatchback, and pump up the volume. We listened to recordings all the way to Toronto and, a few months later, all the way back to Grand Rapids. Many came from the classical repertoire, but some featured Canadian singer songwriters, like Bruce Cockburn and Loreena McKennitt. McKennitt's *An Ancient Muse* became a favorite album. In my mind the track "Penelope's Song," which speaks of faithful waiting for a loved one to return, became Hannah's Song. Sometimes on her behalf I would sing along.

As any parent knows, deepening attachment brings a stronger desire to protect the one you love. This desire became vivid in my dreams during these transitional years. In one dream, recorded in early June 2013, I am in the countryside with Hannah. The area reminds me of Burwood District Cemetery near Escalon, California, where my parents are buried, but without its trees. When I sit down to rest a white coyote appears behind us. Hannah barks and runs toward it, and the coyote runs away. Hannah chases it, as if to play. Suddenly another animal appears and charges at Hannah. It looks like a small mountain lion. Hannah thinks it also wants to play. But I sense danger and cry out. It's too late. The mountain lion attacks, crippling Hannah with one blow. She yelps and writhes away, dragging her hindquarters. I run toward Hannah and the lion, frantically looking for something to throw. I find a rock. Even though my arm feels as if stuck in mud, I hurl it and hit the mountain lion, which backs away. As the lion eyes me the coyote lunges at Hannah. Then I realize I'm in danger too. Yet I continue toward Hannah, trying to scare off the two attackers and calling her. She struggles to get away, but she cannot run. I feel desperate and achingly sad. (That's when I awoke.)

This feeling lingered throughout the day. The next night I had an even more disturbing dream of Hannah being under attack. Nothing in our daily life seemed to trigger such nightmares. They were reverse signs of the strong bond between us, a bond that during our semesters together helped me stay in touch with other people and kept me attuned to the outdoors.

Hannah also countered the absent-mindedness induced by intense academic work in isolation. One drizzly Saturday evening in late November 2014, as I read in our basement apartment with Hannah lying nearby, I felt like having some Scotch and a snack. There were no goodies in the apartment. So I decided to supplement my Scotch with a rice cake, rather Spartan fare. I poured some Scotch, unwrapped a rice cake, and returned to my easy chair. Once seated, I realized I'd left my glass of Scotch across the room. So I got up to fetch it. In the two seconds it took to retrieve my Scotch, Hannah made her move. I turned around to the happy crunch of her chowing down on a rice cake—happy for her, not for me. I did not even bother to reclaim part of it. It was Hannah's reward for my absent-mindedness.

Formed in a time of transitions, my strong bond with Hannah helped me complete many moves: from one country to another, from one musical network to another, from full-time teaching to half-time, and finally from employment to retirement. She also eased the isolation of living alone for several months at a stretch. During the few times when I left her back in Grand Rapids, and on long teaching days in Toronto when I left her alone at the apartment, I could imagine her faithfully waiting, like Penelope for Ulysses, until I returned. Whenever I left her, Hannah's Cleopatra eyes seemed to say: Till you come to me, I'll keep your heart with mine. She was never absent-minded. We had become deeply attached. Her unstinting devotion upheld me during the sometimes lonely sunset of my teaching career.

8

Dusk

And I shall have some peace there, for peace comes dropping slow,
Dropping from the veils of the morning to where the cricket sings;
There midnight's all a glimmer, and noon a purple glow,
And evening full of the linnet's wings.

—William Butler Yeats[10]

Hannah and I did not go camping for her eighth birthday in early July 2015. By then we had established a new place for our outdoor adventures: rather than Awenda Provincial Park in Ontario, now we camped at Lake Michigan Recreation Area in the Manistee National Forest, about 120 miles northwest of Grand Rapids. It had several large, rustic campgrounds, long, forested hiking trails, and miles of pristine Lake Michigan beaches. Nor did we always time our midsummer trip to Hannah's actual birthday, waiting instead for the promise of good weather and few mosquitoes.

    That year we had another reason to wait. At Hannah's annual wellness exam in May I asked her veterinarian to check a small lump I had felt beneath the skin on Hannah's back left flank. Her vet thought it might consist of harmless fat droplets. Yet, as a precaution, she extracted a sample and examined it under a microscope. Her findings confirmed my fears: the test came back positive for cancer. Hannah had basal cell carcinoma in a sweat gland. It would need to be surgically removed.

Dusk

A month later I brought Hannah in for her day of surgery. When I returned eight hours later her left flank sported a six-inch incision, internally sutured, and she wore an Elizabethan collar to keep her from licking it. A few days later the pathology report assured us that the surgery had completely removed the cancerous tumor ("clean margins all around") and that this type of cancer would not migrate to other areas. Joyce and I felt very relieved.

Hannah, however, was not a happy camper. Like most dogs, she hated to wear the "cone of shame." Nor did she understand why we restricted her activities—no rough housing, no long walks, and certainly no running or swimming. These restrictions must have seemed especially stupid because her friend Remy, Toni's little Borador, was staying with us from mid-June until early August while Toni taught in Istanbul. Why have your playmate nearby if you cannot play? Yet the word from Hannah's doctor was final: for the internal sutures to hold and for the incision to heal, Hannah needed to chill. Then after fourteen days the sutures would come out and her normal activities could resume.

Sunday evening, three days after the surgery, to cheer Hannah up and change her scenery, I drove her through the countryside to the Allendale campus of Grand Valley State University (GVSU). Helen Hofmeister, the Minister of Music at Westminster Presbyterian Church and our choir director, gave a carillon concert that evening. Hannah and I sat on the lawn with other concertgoers and listened to the music. It was a lovely concert in the calm evening air. Yet for Hannah it could not compare with our usual weekend hiking and swimming in the state parks along Lake Michigan's shore.

A few more days of restricted activities during Remy's visit made Hannah go stir crazy. One morning after breakfast she rolled over on her back in the carpeted family room, grinning at me, wagging her tail, and vigorously swinging her hindquarters from side to side. How do you keep a healthy, happy, and athletic dog from celebrating a new summer day? I failed to stop her in time. When she stood up, her six-inch incision had broken wide open, exposing the muscles beneath. I felt sick. We'd completely lost the progress Hannah had made toward recovery. I had to take her back for another full-day session at the clinic. This time Hannah showed up in the waiting room with six inches of metal staples lining her left flank. They looked like a misplaced Frankenstein zipper. It would be fourteen days before the staples could be removed.

Needless to say, the time surrounding Hannah's eighth birthday on July 7 was subdued. Joyce and I did take Remy and Hannah out for a car ride in the countryside on the Fourth of July to escape the explosion of fireworks in our own neighborhood. The next day, a Sunday, I took Hannah to another GVSU carillon concert. But camping on her birthday was out of the question.

Hannah's ordeal called up sharp edges of my grief when Rosa died. Until I discovered Hannah's tiny tumor, she had seemed so healthy and vibrant for her age. If I had not felt a small growth when petting her, we would never have discovered that she had localized cancer. I felt badly for our sweet dog. She had no idea why she had been anaesthetized, cut open, sewn up, Elizabethan-collared, and kept from doing most of what she loves to do. I also worried that this marked the beginning of her inevitable decline, whether due to cancer or simply to growing old.

Nevertheless, four days after the staples came out, Hannah and I headed north for three sun-drenched days of camping, hiking, and swimming at Lake Michigan Recreation Area. Despite her recent trauma, eight-year-old Hannah was a pure joy to be with: calm, glad to receive affection but not demanding attention, and as enthusiastic a hiker and swimmer as ever. Even though I would turn sixty-five in less than two weeks, I too felt both youthful energy and a peaceful glow. My classroom teaching had ended in December 2014; Hannah and I had fully settled in Grand Rapids; and I had returned full-time to my first vocational passions: philosophy and music.

On our third evening Hannah and I hiked to the top of a wooden observation deck overlooking the dunes and Lake Michigan. Her feathery coat glistened as she sat on the bench beside me in the goldening sun. We listened for bird songs above and beachgoers below. And we waited for dusk to arrive. As the sun slid downward our future took flight, like a silent sea gull on the darkening horizon. We would welcome a peace that comes dropping slow in evenings full of song and a purple glow.

9

Deep Midnight

"Ich schlief, ich schlief—,	"I was asleep—
Aus tiefem Traum bin ich erwacht:—	From a deep dream I woke and swear:
Die Welt ist tief,	The world is deep,
Und tiefer als der Tag gedacht.	Deeper than day had been aware.
Tief ist ihr Weh—,	Deep is its woe;
Lust—tiefer noch als Herzeleid:	Joy—deeper yet than agony:
Weh spricht: Vergeh!	Woe implores: Go!
Doch alle Lust will Ewigkeit—,	But all joy wants eternity—
—will tiefe, tiefe Ewigkeit!"	Wants deep, wants deep eternity."

—FRIEDRICH NIETZSCHE[11]

HANNAH'S SURGERY IN JUNE 2015 heightened my awareness of her health. Perhaps I should have worried more about my own. In January 2017 I suffered a transient ischemic attack (TIA)—a mini-stroke—and spent seven hours in the emergency ward at Blodgett Hospital. Multiple tests and consultations in the next few months determined that I had two underlying heart conditions, never detected before, that could trigger another attack at any time. I began to take three heart-related medications. In combination they often made me woozy. More than a half year would pass before the wooziness disappeared. The entire experience unnerved me, as if the ground of good health on which my singing and writing rested had randomly earthquaked away.

An even greater upheaval awaited. Not long after Hannah's tenth birthday in July 2017 she became more reluctant to go on daily walks in the neighborhood. She had never been an eager sidewalk stroller, much preferring to ride in the car or run free, but she still loved our big hikes every weekend as well as vigorous play with other dogs. Increasingly, however, I had to coax her to walk around the block. I thought the issue was psychological, a trauma of some sort. Perhaps her old fear of fireworks was taking over. Or maybe the aggressive barks of a neighbor's German Shepherd intimidated her. Hannah did not limp or seem stiff. I could not explain her resistance to routine walking.

A few months later I began to notice an odd trembling in her right hind leg during our long hikes on the weekend. Whenever she stopped to look around or listen, her leg would begin to shake, almost as if she were chilled, even on the hottest days. I asked about this at her next visit to the veterinary clinic in December 2017, but the vet said Hannah's limbs and nervous system seemed fine.

Within two months, Hannah began to limp noticeably. She would struggle to stand and then avoid putting weight on her right hind leg until she had walked a few paces. I took her back to the clinic. Though the vet who examined her could not find anything abnormal, he suspected she had developed arthritis. So he recommended Hannah lose some weight, moderate her activities, and begin an anti-inflammatory medication. We followed his advice. By the time of Hannah's annual wellness exam in June 2018 she was less noticeably lame and five pounds lighter (although she had never been overweight). The vet did note a pained response to pressure on Hannah's hips, however. At her suggestion we started to enrich Hannah's meals with a fish oil supplement. Like anything fishy, she really loved it!

At the beginning of August 2018 Joyce and I traveled to California for ten days to visit family members and friends and to attend my fiftieth high school class reunion. It was my first time back since my mom's funeral in 2009. The night before our flight to San Francisco we brought Hannah to stay with our friends Becky and

Steve. They lived in a lovely home on an inland lake, a perfect setting for our water dog. Hannah had stayed with them before and they enjoyed her company.

The day after we returned from California Becky and Steve drove into Grand Rapids to bring Hannah back. As soon as she got out of their car, I noticed she was limping more awkwardly than when we had left. But I thought it was a temporary discomfort that would soon pass. To celebrate our being back together, the next day, a Saturday, I drove Hannah out to Saugatuck Dunes State Park for a long hike and a vigorous swim.

Clearly I had misread Hannah's signals. When I went downstairs to fix breakfast the next morning, she did not follow. Even though I had put fish-oil-doused food in her bowl, she stayed at the top of the stairs, wanting to descend but unable to try. So I walked back upstairs and carried her down. When I set Hannah near her food bowl, she could barely stand—I had to prop her up as she ate. All day Hannah found it hard to stand and walk. It being a Sunday, her veterinary clinic was closed. The hours crawled by. I could not bear to see her suffer and not know why.

The next day Hannah and I spent two hours at the clinic. After a thorough physical exam, blood tests, and radiographs, she was diagnosed with osteosarcoma, an aggressive bone cancer, in her right hind leg. Two days later we brought Hannah to a veterinary oncologist who confirmed the diagnosis. The oncologist also detected arthritis in the *left* hind leg, and she suggested that X-rays might show a partial fracture to the femur (thigh bone) of Hannah's right hind leg. So Hannah had been hobbling awkwardly not only because she felt arthritic pain but also because the bone had deteriorated and possibly fractured. Moreover, her leg muscles had atrophied as she avoided putting weight on her right hind foot, and we faced a risk that her femur would break badly, causing even more severe pain.

Joyce and I were devastated. When we had left on vacation two weeks earlier, we never imagined that our dear Hannah was seriously ill. Now we confronted seemingly impossible decisions on behalf of a beloved dog who could not tell us what she would prefer. One option was to amputate the entire leg, followed by chemotherapy. Another was to use radiation treatments to numb the tumor-induced pain. Still another option—for comfort, not for cure—would be a series of drug-infusion treatments, perhaps in combination with chemotherapy. Regardless of which path we chose we knew that cancers like this are nearly always fatal. Even when removed by amputation they usually show up somewhere else: in 95 percent of dogs with osteosarcoma the cancer has already undetectably metastasized by the time they are diagnosed. Even the most aggressive treatments would likely give Hannah only another year to live. Did we want to put her through such trauma with so little prospect of recovery?

We needed another expert opinion. The next day we consulted with a veterinarian from Heaven at Home, an in-home pet hospice service. Dr. Amy Hoss came to our house and spent nearly two hours in our family room getting to know Hannah and discussing treatment options, pain management, and end-of-life care. Being on new pain medications, Hannah was lethargic when Dr. Hoss arrived. But after an hour of conversation, when Dr. Hoss began the physical exam, Hannah rolled onto her back to flash her endearing grin, complete with wagging tail, to our relief and delight. With Dr. Hoss's help we decided not to pursue any of the expensive and invasive treatments the oncologist had laid out. Instead we would do all we could to keep Hannah comfortable until her life ended. When that time arrived, Dr. Hoss would come to our house for in-home euthanasia.

Living out such an irreversible decision can be just as difficult as the decision itself. The new prescriptions to control Hannah's pain made her even more woozy than my heart medications had made me. The first few days she lost interest in food and seemed restless. Lying down was difficult, and getting up even harder. Hannah would whimper and utter deep moaning sighs. But when I stroked her tired body, that seemed to soothe her, and she would lie peacefully for a time, with a fan blowing gently across her and caressing her light golden hair.

All of our daily patterns changed. For the first two weeks I abandoned my normal second-floor office work and set up shop in the first-floor family room, where Hannah liked to lie. There I journaled and wrote email. I also read about her disease, dietary suggestions, exercise options, and preparations for death. We no longer went for daily walks around the block. Instead I would lift Hannah into the car and drive her to Pleasant Park a few blocks away, where we could walk and she could do her business. Then we would sit on the shaded grass while I talked with Hannah, sang and hummed songs, and told her I loved her. Eventually she would roll over on one side, her eyes nearly shut, in relaxation and contentment.

Such moments of grace helped ease my own pain. Still, how could I watch Hannah suffer and know I could do little to prevent it or to prolong her life? How could I face losing this gentle, affectionate, and lovely dog to whom I was so deeply attached? With every inch of my mostly healthy body I wanted to cry out "Weh spricht: vergeh!" Pain and suffering implore to be removed, just as joy and gladness call out to continue. Yet I knew only Hannah's death would fully remove her suffering, and I could feel neither joy nor gladness about that. I felt dark sorrow, midnight sorrow, sorrow nearly as deep as the joy of our lifelong bond.

10

Zigzag

> I will arise and go now, for always night and day
> I hear lake water lapping with low sounds by the shore;
> While I stand on the roadway, or on the pavements grey,
> I hear it in the deep heart's core.
>
> —WILLIAM BUTLER YEATS[12]

HOW DO YOU PREPARE for the death of a dog you love? Will she be ready to leave when the time comes? How do you decide when to say goodbye? What right do we have to decide? In the days after the hospice veterinarian first visited my questions chased each other round and round, like unruly dogs at mutant play. Why did I so trustingly accept the diagnosis of arthritis a half year earlier? Why didn't I clue into the signal of her leg's trembling when Hannah stood still? When did her bone cancer start? Could we have sought effective treatments earlier? My questions kept swirling. Even though several vets assured us that an aggressive cancer like this might have started undetectably only a few months before, I felt responsible for Hannah's suffering.

Reading the right books and talking with close friends helped shift my perspective. So did Hannah's complete trust in my caregiving. After accepting that I could not have prevented her illness, I decided to do all I could to help her live well. But what does living well mean for a beautiful and athletic dog hobbled by bone cancer, arthritis, and the resulting pain? Dr. Hoss, the hospice veterinarian, gave us a "Quality of Life Scale" with seven criteria and made suggestions about how to score each one.[13] The day after her in-home visit I created a chart called "Hannah's Quality of Life Scale" and began to measure daily signs of health and happiness, noting circumstances that might affect particular scores. Well aware that either misplaced empathy or wishful thinking could cloud my judgment, I nevertheless hoped the sequence of daily scores would show trends of improvement or deterioration. Eventually they might help us decide when it was time to say goodbye.

The Heaven at Home Pet Hospice also loaned us a Help Em Up Harness to make it easier to navigate our stairs at home and to lift Hannah into and out of the car. We used this for the first few weeks, until it became clear that Hannah preferred to negotiate the stairs on her own, relying on my supportive hand, and would rather have me physically hug-lift her into the car and out again.

Did Hannah's handicap mean she might never swim again? All the Lake Michigan parks where we usually went on the weekends required long hikes or steep stairways to get to the water—more than she should try now. Because Hannah and I loved to swim, I dreaded giving this up. So I went online to search for a suitable and accessible dog beach. To my surprise I found one called Kruse Park, about an hour's drive from Grand Rapids.

On the first Sunday afternoon after receiving Hannah's diagnosis, she and I drove out to explore Norman F. Kruse Park, a Muskegon city park on the shoreline of Lake Michigan. Rather than take the steep stairway down, we zigzagged along the park's gently sloping and handicapped-accessible boardwalk toward a large and relaxed array of dogs and people. Because the beach was not wide, Hannah did not need to cross much sand to get to the lake. Once we neared the water I removed her Help Em Up Harness. Hannah promptly hobbled into Lake Michigan and settled into it to the tips of her ears, a sign of pure pleasure. Then she began to walk around in the shallow water.

After letting her roam for a while I too waded into the water, Hannah paddling alongside. Then we went for an extended swim together, out into the lake, back toward the shore, out again, parallel to the shore, and around and around, with Hannah using all four limbs, including her arthritic, cancerous, and atrophied right hind leg. She so loved the sheer joy of swimming, without anything to fetch, just being together in the water. Eventually we returned to shore. I sat down on a towel to dry off and Hannah perched herself right in front of me, observing the other dogs and people nearby and showing no anxiety. After soaking up the sun, we zigzagged back up to the car, not using the harness, and then enjoyed a leisurely drive home.

Kruse Park became our regular weekend destination for the next two months until the weather turned colder. On Sunday of the following week we drove there again. Hannah was eager to get to the water. Once in, she swam and swam, occasionally looking at the other dogs around her, but mostly reveling in her own little water world. Soon I joined her, and we swam together for a long time. Then I threw a stick, and she bounded into the water after it, not as vigorously as in her pre-cancerous prime, yet just as intently. But bounding was not good exercise. So I encouraged Hannah to keep swimming with her stick rather than dropping it for another round of fetching. Eventually I called her out of the water, and again we sat on the beach to watch the other people and dogs. Hannah showed great interest even as she contentedly sat there, pressed against my legs, to oversee the activity around her. Quietly we listened to the lake water lapping.

The next week Joyce joined Hannah and me for another Sunday afternoon outing to Kruse Park. After observing Hannah's swimming with me, a couple on the beach asked us about her. When we described her condition, they said they had started all three of their Golden Retrievers on raw meat and encouraged us to try this with Hannah. That evening I immediately placed an online order for high-quality frozen meat meals delivered door-to-door. It was expensive, but we wanted to do whatever we could, short of drastic interventions, to maintain Hannah's quality of life. We did not seek miraculous cures—just relief from pain and ongoing restoration of Hannah's gentle and playful spirit.

Joyce and I also received support from others. Around the same time as the first trip to Kruse Park I received a phone call from our friend Dan, a naturopathic doctor who knows a lot about alternative medicine. Dan told me about his friend David, whose Fox Red Labrador named Amber had had liver cancer. After receiving Amber's diagnosis, David switched her to a raw meat diet and used marijuana to help control her symptoms. Amber had lived two years longer than predicted, two good years, until she died in 2017. Dan explained why this diet and medication might have helped.

I don't believe in magic. Yet I am open to nontraditional approaches, whether in philosophy, music, or life. Encouraged by Amber's story and Dan's explanations, I called David. He invited Hannah and me to meet him at his home in the countryside. We drove out there after supper that evening and had a pleasant visit. David was so sweet with Hannah; she clearly liked meeting him. He told me more of Amber's story. He also explained how he had prepared the marijuana for her use. Then he generously gave us the rest of Amber's supply. The next day Hannah started her nontraditional medication.

Two weeks later we discontinued the marijuana. When I called Hannah's primary vet to refill two prescriptions for pain and gave her an update, the vet warned that marijuana can be toxic for dogs. So, reluctantly, I pulled Hannah off it. Then a week later, based on more research, I started Hannah on CBD oil, a marijuana derivate that does not contain THC, marijuana's potentially toxic psychoactive ingredient. Now I would have to observe whether her taking CBD oil made any noticeable difference.

That's how the first few weeks unfolded after Hannah's diagnosis. It was like stumbling back and forth blindfolded in a guessing game. I could not see what was happening to the bones and muscles in her damaged leg, and she could not use words to tell me how she felt. Every trace of discomfort—Hannah's whimpering, lethargy, or restlessness—added to my sorrow. Each sign of improvement—her enjoyment of visitors, unexpected playfulness, or eagerness to swim—sparked a quiet celebration. One day she could seem weary and bored at Pleasant Park; the next day, if young children fawned over her, she would happily trot after her frisbee, shake it up, and bring it back. Her restless whining in the morning could yield by suppertime to several indoor rounds of Find the Squeaker-Toy.

My emotional zigzag continued day by day. How could I even hope that Hannah's good days would outnumber poor ones in the weeks ahead? Yet, thanks to support from others and the gift of Kruse Park, beyond the zigzag Hannah and I could hear lake water lapping. We could hear it lapping with low sounds by the shore. We could hear it in the deep heart's core.

11

Cradle Song

> Die zeigen im Traum   May they show you in a dream
> Dir Christkindleins Baum   The infant Christ child's tree.
> Schlaf nun selig und süß   Go to sleep, blest and sweet,
> Schau im Traums Paradies   See the joy of your dream.
>
> —Brahms's "Lullaby"

Although the Quality of Life Scale helped me track Hannah's wellbeing, it did not register my own. How do you measure your own distress and sorrow? I quickly lost motivation for my usual scholarly work. I canceled some smaller obligations, struggled to write a conference response to papers on one of my recent books, and temporarily abandoned work on a large new book about truth, my primary research project. At the two philosophy conferences I attended in September and October I felt awkwardly detached from both the topics and the people debating them. When the adult choir at Westminster Presbyterian Church and the Chamber Choir of Grand Rapids resumed rehearsals in early September, I felt little of my usual joy in singing, despite the engaging repertoire.

Hannah's unexpected illness had sapped my spirit; I couldn't shake a sense of constant sadness. She did her best to help me out—trotting after her frisbee outdoors, sometimes acting silly indoors

To Sing Once More

(grinning at us upside down while wagging her tail remained a favorite), even struggling upstairs unbidden and unassisted to visit me in my second-floor office. In fact, by late September and early October her quality of life scores had definitely improved. Thanks to her pain medicines, raw meat diet, CBD oil, swimming, and our other efforts, she was doing amazingly well. Yet I could not help thinking every day, This won't last. When will Hannah's thigh bone, perhaps partially fractured already, break more severely? When will she lose all use of her damaged leg? When will the cancer migrate to her lungs? When will we need to say our last goodbye?

That's when I learned just how synchronized Hannah's wellbeing was to my own. I became overly busy in early September when a local philosophy conference occupied many hours every day, and Hannah's quality of life scores sank. Her whimpering and restlessness each morning indicated both more pain and less happiness. After I attended a philosophy conference at Penn State University a month later, Hannah's condition declined again, compared with the good days before I had left: her hobbling became more pronounced, and her whining resumed for several days. Indirectly, then, Hannah's quality of life scores tracked my own wellbeing: they reflected how attentive I had been to her needs. I resolved to be more fully present for her in however many weeks and months remained.

Singing to Hannah helped. During the first week after her diagnosis, as I sat with her in the family room, we often listened to the "Lullabies" stream on YourClassical.org. I also played a CD that ends with a lovely arrangement of the Brahms's "Lullaby" or "Wiegenlied" (Cradle Song), sung in the original German, with piano and clarinet accompaniment.[14] This simple, honest music—both a plea and a benediction—spoke directly not only to my desire for healing but also to my need to gently let Hannah go. I printed the German lyrics and tucked them into my billfold. From then on when Hannah and I sat together, whether indoors or outside, and no one else was around, I would hum the melody and sometimes sing her the "Wiegenlied," using the more poetic and spiritually attuned German lyrics rather than the standard English versions:

Guten Abend, gut' Nacht	Lullaby and good night!
Mit Rosen bedacht	Draped with roses' delight,
Mit Näglein besteckt	With carnations adorned,
Schlupf unter die Deck	May the covers keep you warm.
Morgen früh, wenn Gott will	Come the dawn, if God wills,
Wirst du wieder geweckt	You shall wake up once more.
Morgen früh, wenn Gott will	Come the dawn, if God wills,
Wirst du wieder geweckt	You shall wake up once more.
Guten Abend, gut' Nacht	Lullaby and good night!
Von Englein bewacht	As the angels alight,
Die zeigen im Traum	May they show you in a dream
Dir Christkindleins Baum	The infant Christ child's tree.
Schlaf nun selig und süß	Go to sleep, blest and sweet,
Schau im Traums Paradies	See the joy of your dream.
Schlaf nun selig und süß	Go to sleep, blest and sweet,
Schau im Traums Paradies[15]	See the joy of your dream.

Hannah loved to be sung to, especially when I sat on the ground beside her and stroked her silky sides. I could find no purer way to express my affection and my promise to stay attentive to her needs: *Schlaf nun selig und süß / Schau im Traums Paradies* (Go to sleep, blest and sweet, / See the joy of your dream).

    Visits with friends also lifted our spirits. Hannah remained as eager as ever to welcome visitors at the front door, even though she took longer to get there and her greetings were lower key. And her friend Remy, the Border Collie Lab mix, stayed with us when Toni had long days at the university. Not long after my conference in Pennsylvania, when Hannah's wellness scores had dropped, Remy stayed with us for two days. At noon on the first day I put Hannah and Remy in the back of our Toyota Matrix and drove them to Pleasant Park a few blocks down the street. While Hannah roamed freely, I walked Remy around on his leash so he could take care of business without distractions. (Despite his congested lungs, he energetically chased squirrels and rabbits whenever he could.) Meanwhile I tossed a rubber ball for Hannah to saunter after and bring back.

    Eventually I released Remy as well. Instantly his hunting instincts kicked in, and he excitedly dashed after Hannah's ball.

Because of Hannah's handicap, Remy had no trouble getting to it first. But, unlike Hannah, he was more a hunter and herder than a retriever. He showed little interest in bringing the ball back. When he dropped it many yards away from us, Hannah gingerly meandered over and picked it up. Then, as if to say, "Brother Remy, this is how it's done," she walked back and deposited the ball at my feet, looking, of course, for a treat, which I gladly gave her. At that point Remy clued in and came for his own treat. Then I'd throw the ball again. Away Remy would tear while Hannah patiently waited for another chance to demonstrate his failure at Retrieval 101. Their tag-team antics made me laugh.

Yet sadness tinged my smiles, like the hint of melancholy lacing Brahms's "Lullaby." I could pray the covers would keep us warm until we wake once more, but I knew one morning Hannah would not rise to greet the dawn. I could sing her to sleep, sweet and blest, and pray the angels to guide her, but I could not see the paradise of joy that I asked her to dream. What we pursue in our lullabies we cannot always retrieve.

12

Nightmare

> When I am laid, am laid in earth, May my wrongs create
> No trouble, no trouble in thy breast;
> Remember me, remember me, but ah! forget my fate.
> Remember me, but ah! forget my fate.
>
> —Purcell, "Dido's Lament"[16]

Hannah's spirit and gait seemed to improve as the weather cooled in early November 2018. She whimpered and hobbled less, and she showed renewed energy outdoors. One day she played with a puppy at Pleasant Park, rolling onto her back to let it "win." Another day, when our neighbor Pat walked over to our backyard to say hello, Hannah scampered about as if *she* were the puppy.

But in late November, right after American Thanksgiving, Hannah's condition dramatically declined. Preoccupied by two concert performances that weekend with the Chamber Choir of Grand Rapids, I made a rare but costly mistake. On Saturday night I brought Hannah up to our bedroom as usual, tucked her into her kennel with her stuffed dog, Estelle, and we went to sleep. Several hours later Hannah started to whine. It was around 3:30 early Sunday morning. Thinking she needed to go outside, I got up and brought her downstairs. She hobbled out to our backyard for a bathroom break and came back in. Although Hannah was reluctant to return to our second-floor bedroom, I carried her upstairs and tried to help her get comfortable on a dog blanket outside her kennel.

Hannah could not settle. She kept getting up, turning around, and trying again to lie down, whining off and on. Usually she did not complain at night, so I knew she was in pain. Suddenly I realized my mistake: I had forgotten to give Hannah her pain pill and CBD oil before bedtime. Quickly I went downstairs to get them, brought them up, and gave them to her. But Hannah kept whining, and I did not want us to disturb Joyce's sleep. So I coaxed Hannah back downstairs and let her outside on the back deck, where increasingly she liked to lie when she was uncomfortable. Eventually I called her inside. She lay down in the family room, and I read myself to sleep there for a few more hours.

I felt awful about forgetting Hannah's medications. I also wondered whether this awake-in-slow-motion nightmare marked a new stage in her suffering and demise. Looking back, I can say that it did. Even though I strengthened the dosage for one of her two pain medications, Hannah showed increasing discomfort each day thereafter. Mornings were especially bad. For the next several days she would start to whine after breakfast and ask to go outside. Once in the backyard she would burrow into our dying dune grasses and lie there for hours at a time. Within a week she lost interest in eating, often leaving half of her breakfast untouched until nearly noon. By Friday, December 7, two weeks after Thanksgiving, I felt overwhelmed by Hannah's deterioration. I called her hospice veterinarian. Dr. Hoss listened carefully, prescribed a third pain medication, and promised to visit us on Monday, December 10.

The morning of Dr. Hoss's visit came after another rough night. Hannah's whining awakened me at 3:15 AM. When I took her downstairs she immediately went outside. Snow covered the ground, but that didn't matter. Hannah wanted to lie in the snow. After an hour she came back inside. I gave her half of the new pain pill Dr. Hoss had prescribed on Friday, and we caught an hour of sleep in the family room. Then Hannah resumed her whining, and I administered her other two pain medications for the morning. Again she wanted to go outside, where she stayed for two hours, sleeping in the snow. Finally, she came in to eat a bit but left most of her breakfast uneaten. Then she fell asleep in the family room, waking up and finishing her breakfast right before Dr. Hoss arrived at 11:30.

Dr. Hoss took her time to pet Hannah, talk with us, and thoroughly examine her. She agreed that Hannah's condition had markedly declined and she was in a lot of pain. She also determined that the tumor in Hannah's leg had grown significantly. Dr. Hoss advised us to increase the dosages of Hannah's pain medications and see whether that brought some relief. But she also asked us to consider scheduling in-home euthanasia.

So began what I came to call "Hannah's Last 12 Days," from December 10 to 21. I stayed with her throughout every day and took extensive notes all day long about her activities and symptoms. The pattern of restlessness and discomfort worsened. At night Hannah no longer used her kennel—I worried she would be trapped in it if her leg snapped. She slept on dog blankets next to our bed, with Estelle nearby. About half of each day Hannah lay by herself outdoors in the cold on our wooden deck or on the snow-covered lawn or among the pressed-down dune grasses. She would lie outside several hours at a time, beginning right after we came downstairs in the morning and continuing intermittently throughout the day. When she came inside she often whimpered or whined and seemed unable to settle in any one place for long. Joyce and I tried to comfort her with massages, lullabies, and belly rubs, and we gave her specially flavored treats to chew, but these afforded only fleeting solace.

Occasionally Hannah would show her old spirit: retrieving her ball at Pleasant Park during our noontime outings there, or vigorously shaking her rope toy after coming inside. But with her frequent requests to lie alone outside, and her inability to settle indoors, I felt she was preparing to leave us. After talking with our friend Toni, who came over for supper a few days after Dr. Hoss's visit, Joyce and I decided the time had come to say goodbye. I emailed Dr. Hoss. She agreed to come to our house one last time on the following Friday, December 21.

Reaching this decision felt like a permanently looping bad dream. I was relieved that one uncertainty had disappeared—the uncertainty of when Hannah would die. But I did not want the new certainty; I hated making the worst decision a dog's companion can be forced into; I felt both unprepared to lose Hannah and unsuited to assist her dying. It was a nightmare from which, while dreaming it, I knew I could not wake up.

The next afternoon, a Saturday, Joyce and I drove with Hannah to our friends Connie and Darlene's house so they and Mazie, their Miniature Goldendoodle, could say their goodbyes. On the way there Joyce wondered aloud whether we had made our decision about euthanasia too hastily. Hannah still seemed so healthy, she said, and so "alive" in many ways. I reviewed our reasons not to delay: the risk of serious injury and pain, the marked and measurable decline in Hannah's wellbeing, and my own stress and exhaustion as the primary caregiver. My last reason felt selfish, but I needed to say it. Caring for a loved one who suffers creates its own anguish and fatigue.

Mazie greeted Hannah enthusiastically when we arrived. They roamed from room to room, Hannah exploring unfamiliar territory and Mazie trying to distract her into playing. Then all of us settled in the living room. Joyce and I brought our friends up to date about Hannah's condition. We told them that Dr. Hoss would come to our house to administer euthanasia on the next Friday, the Winter Solstice. Connie and Darlene gave us warm hugs as we left, and Connie took pictures of Joyce and me on either side of Hannah as she looked out our car's rear window.

Afterward the three of us drove to Seidman Park, a favorite spot to hike with Hannah in the countryside east of Grand Rapids. It was a gray, overcast afternoon. Most of the recent snow had melted. Wet brown leaves coated the trails and forest floor. We walked a short and easy path together. When we reached the rough-hewn bench where I usually sat with Hannah, she stood near us to be petted. Then she lay down on a blanket of leaves as Joyce and I sat nearby. We told Hannah she's a great dog. We hummed Brahms's "Wiegenlied" together. I recited both verses. Then we walked back to the car, and I lifted Hannah into the back to leave. "This was our last time together at Seidman, Pups," I said. But to Joyce I murmured, "I'll be back here, alone."

Nightmare

    Alone, but not fully alone. Through the nightmare haze of our decision I could already hear, like Dido's crushingly sad lament, Hannah's spirit calling: Remember me, remember me, but ah forget my fate. Do not let the tragedy of a loved one's life cut short blot out your memories of her. Do not forget the dream dog who, from the day of her adoption, you held close. May my suffering create no trouble in your soul when I am gone. You will not walk alone. I'll remain in your heart.

13

Farewell

> It now leads onward
> And I know not where
> I feel in my heart
> That you will be there
> Whenever a storm comes
> Whatever our fears
> The journey goes on
> As your love ever nears
>
> —Loreena McKennitt[17]

ONCE YOU KNOW WHEN your dog will die, every minute becomes precious. While I sat in the family room, letting Hannah in and out as she requested and trying to maintain her routines of food and medicine, I began to sort through hundreds and hundreds of photos we had taken of her over more than eleven years. I reflected on our life together. I read about end-of-life ceremonies. And I planned special non-stress afternoon outings to say farewell at our favorite spots in West Michigan: Norman F. Kruse Park on Sunday, and then, on each subsequent afternoon, Saugatuck Dunes State Park, Aman Park, Pleasant Park, and Aquinas College. During the first three outings, which required longer trips, I sang to Hannah in the car and put on some of our favorite CDs.

Farewell

Sunday afternoon, December 16, 2018, was overcast but not cold. We arrived at Kruse Park around 2:00 PM. First Hannah and I walked the zigzagging boardwalk down to the beach, where I let her off her leash. Unlike our visits in the late summer and early fall, hardly anyone else was around. As Hannah explored the beach's smells, we walked slowly north for a hundred yards. When she did not go to the lake, I found a place away from the water where we could rest. I sat down and Hannah stood nearby, looking around and listening while I took many photographs of her.

Then I sang her the Brahms "Wiegenlied," her lullaby. "Hannah, you are a fine retriever and a wonderful companion," I said. "Thank you for making my loneliness not lonely anymore."

By this time Hannah had laid down on the sand and I could stroke her as I sang and talked. Then we got up and walked in the other direction. Now Hannah limped toward the water and, true to her life's passion, she waded in. Next she waded back out and flopped down for a vigorous roll on a clump of washed-up dune grasses, her back on the wet sand, all four legs flailing. Then she flipped over and struggled to her feet. Despite her extreme discomfort in recent days, she had not lost her joyous spirit.

For the last stage of this farewell visit we walked up the boardwalk to a fallen tree in the dune grasses above the beach and lake. There we sat again, looking out at Lake Michigan. Restless at first, Hannah calmed down when people and dogs emerged on the beach below. She observed them intently and I took more photographs. Just as we were getting ready to leave, a man started to fly a wooden model airplane along the dunes. It swung close to where we sat and then back again. This quietly gliding "bird," whose wings never flapped, fascinated Hannah. She followed its flight back and forth as the plane flew past her gaze through the lake-reflected sunlight. In the magic of this moment I said, "Hannah, that's how your spirit will soar on Friday, free as a bird, not hobbling, without pain. You'll have a new life. Maybe one day I'll find you, and we can swim together, swim and swim, just as we used to."

Two days later, on Tuesday, our long goodbye took us to Aman Park, a large forested park in the countryside west of Grand Rapids. Hannah was reluctant to walk the trail from the parking lot even though I had let her off the leash. I had to call her many times, retrace my steps, and give her extra encouragement—quite unlike the days when Hannah would eagerly trot ahead, sometimes exploring so far off the trail that I'd have to call her back. We went only a short distance, to a bench overlooking a downward slope to other trails. There we stayed, Hannah standing or lying down and I sitting on the bench.

As we rested I told Hannah about my going to the Humane Society of West Michigan in September 2006, the first time I looked for another dog after Rosa died. I told Hannah how hard it was to see all the homeless dogs that day and not feel up to adopting one. Afterward I came to Aman Park to sit on a bank overlooking Sand Creek and reflect on the death-shaped hole in my heart. But then one year later, on August 31, 2007, our little Hannah Estelle came home to live with us, brightening my life with her affection and playfulness and beauty.

Before leaving, I took photographs of Hannah on her sun-dappled blanket of fallen leaves, sunlight and shadows accenting her golden loveliness. I couldn't get enough of looking at her; I marveled at her beauty, even with her atrophied leg and crippled gait. Then Hannah eagerly ambled ahead of me all the way back to the car, stopping only a couple of times to sniff a bush or fallen tree limb, and I lifted her into the hatchback where she always traveled.

Once on the road back to Grand Rapids I played Loreena McKennitt's "Penelope's Song" and "Never-Ending Road," calling back to Hannah, "Pups, these songs are for you!" Hannah sat up through both tracks as if to listen better. During the instrumental coda to "Never-Ending Road," I watched her in the rearview mirror. She gazed ahead at me, resting her chin atop the back seat, as if to say, "Here is my heart, and I give it to you. Take me with you, where'er you go; hold my dreams in the palm of your hands." We may have concluded the Aman stage of our slow farewell, but not our never-ending road.

The next day I drove Hannah to Pleasant Park for one last afternoon visit. This had become our daily go-to park in the neighborhood, especially after Hannah stopped doing walks around the block and I needed to drive her somewhere to stroll. The day was almost balmy. Hannah willingly walked into the park, but she showed no interest in retrieving her frisbee. So I called her over to me on the slope of the park's east end, where I sat on the grass. She settled nearby. As I stroked her soft, flowing fur, I told her, if I had a choice, I'd do it all over again. I would adopt this adorable little round puppy, train her, accompany her on countless outings to many different dog parks, beaches, and homes, and, in all of this, share her love and friendship. Then, still stroking Hannah, I sang her lullaby.

When I got up, I asked Hannah if she wanted to fetch her frisbee, and she did—twice, once for her and once for me. On the third throw the frisbee stayed where it had landed. I walked over to pick it up. Then we left the park, Hannah hobbling behind me and trotting to catch up, until I put her on the leash and guided her to the car.

The next morning, while Hannah lay outside and Joyce was away, I decided to read aloud several poems and songs that had sustained me in recent months. I started with "The Rainbow Bridge." It's not a sophisticated poem. Many consider it trite or sentimental. But as I read it, my voice began to crack. By the end I was crying uncontrollably, just like I had at my first vocal workshop more than eleven years earlier, on the day before Hannah's birth. Now suddenly, out of nowhere, I had another complete meltdown, on the day before Hannah would die. I sobbed and sobbed as I imagined Hannah after her death, playing, no longer in pain, no longer in sadness, playing and waiting until that glad day when her favorite human arrives and, reunited at last, we cross the rainbow bridge together. In that image lie the love we feel and the hope—inexplicable, mysterious, and outrageous—of life-restoring resurrection. My efforts in philosophy and music are sustained by that hope. But so also, I now realized, was my willingness, however reluctant, to let Hannah go.

That afternoon, before supper, I brushed Hannah and combed out some tangled fur below her ears. After supper Joyce and I bathed her with special hypoallergenic wipes and brushed her again. She enjoyed the special attention. Now she was ready for Dr. Hoss's visit the next morning.

But I felt lost. Our special outings had ended. Our last evening together had arrived. How should we spend it? I lit three candles on the family room coffee table and put favorite Christmas music on the stereo. Hannah stretched out and slept on the floor between the stereo and my recliner as I thought about our ceremony the next day and Joyce wrote a special letter of farewell to Hannah.

Around 8:00 PM Hannah wanted to go outside. It was mild out, under a covering of clouds. Hannah and I settled on the back deck, she lying down, and I sitting on the top step to pet her as I sang her lullaby. Then Joyce opened the French doors a crack so we could hear the CD *An Ancient Muse* playing on the stereo. By then Hannah had stretched out on her side. I lay next to her, stroking her and whispering once in a while, as we listened. The CD ended around 9:00 PM. When I asked Hannah if she wanted to go inside, she was ready. We came in, and she went right to her dog blanket in the family room.

Our last CD for the evening was *A Quiet Place* by the Vancouver Chamber Choir. As their music of healing played, I thought: Hannah has had a good life. I want to hold onto that, without regrets about the good years I had hoped we would still enjoy together. After tomorrow morning our road will lead onward. I might not know where. But deep in my heart, I'll feel she's still there. Despite all our sorrows, whatever our fears, our journey goes on, as love ever nears.

14

Journey's End

> Deep in the winter
> Amidst falling snow
> High in the air
> Where the bells they all toll
> And now all around me
> I feel you still here
> Such is the journey
> No mystery to fear
>
> —Loreena McKennitt[18]

THE DAY OF HANNAH'S midwinter departure arrived: December 21, 2018, the Winter Solstice, the shortest day of the year and the longest night. It was drizzling when Hannah and I got up, but by 9:00 AM the rain had cleared. Joyce had freshened the house and turned on our seasonal decorative lights, and I had lit candles and put on soft violin and lute music by Bach. Shortly after 9:00 AM our dear friend Toni arrived. Hannah was a little puppy when she first met Toni. They always had a special bond. Even as a mature dog, Hannah would squeal with delight when Toni greeted her. This day was no different. After Toni hugged us, she and Hannah had their lovefest on the family room floor.

Then Hannah moved to a larger clearing on the family room carpet, where she stretched out on her left side. Toni and Joyce sat alongside to brush her and to talk to her. Hannah enjoyed this, calmly receiving their affection. I tried, in a tear-shaken voice, to say how much Hannah means to me and how much I love her. Then I joined Joyce and Toni on the floor to groom Hannah and pet her and tell her again how wonderful a companion she has been.

Just after 10:00 AM, as expected, the doorbell rang. It was Dr. Amy Hoss from the Heaven at Home Pet Hospice. When I let Amy in, Hannah came over to greet her. Amy asked how Hannah had been doing. I replied that the various medications had stabilized her pain: Hannah had not whined during the past few nights, although she had been restless every day. Amy immediately noted that Hannah favored her cancerous leg even more than the last time she saw her: Hannah's foot was pointed down, as if in balletic en pointe, and she did not put any weight on it.

We moved into the family room. Hannah stretched out where she had lain before Amy arrived. After completing some paperwork, Amy and I joined Joyce and Toni on the carpet, with Hannah at the center of our circle. We pet her and gently talked to her and reminded one another, in Amy's words, that Hannah is a beautiful soul.

At that point Joyce read a richly textured letter she had written to Hannah the night before,[19] followed by the text of "Hannah's Song," an adaptation of "Penelope's Song." While Joyce read her letter, Toni interjected some of Hannah's endearing mischief, such as raiding waste baskets and snatching up Kleenex. Then I sang Hannah the Brahms "Wiegenlied," petting her all the while, with Joyce humming in harmony. Amy was wonderfully attentive to our need to say a slow farewell. And Hannah was unusually peaceful throughout, almost as if she knew our improvised ceremony was our last goodbye.

Now the time had come. Amy moved to get her kit. She described each step, assuring us that Hannah would feel no pain. With Joyce's help Amy slid a white protective pad under Hannah's hindquarters. Then she injected a powerful sedative between Hannah's shoulders. Over the course of five minutes Hannah became deeply drowsy. She leaned her head against my leg, showing complete trust in my caregiving. Eventually she closed her eyes and began to snore softly. We arranged Estelle, Hannah's lifelong littermate, against her chest. Despite her sedated slumber Hannah's nose twitched, and she stuck out her tongue, as if to lick Estelle and recall once more the distant memory of her mother's scent. Joyce tucked Estelle under Hannah's right front paw, in an embrace. Hannah was fast asleep, *im Traums Paradies* (in the paradise of dreams).

Then Amy described how she would administer euthanasia. After covering Hannah's hindquarters with a purple blanket, she shaved a patch of fur off Hannah's damaged leg and carefully tucked it into a Ziploc bag for us to keep. Then she injected the lethal drugs. We waited, stroking Hannah and telling her our love. After a few minutes Amy placed her stethoscope on Hannah's chest. She listened, and said, "She's gone."

I couldn't believe it. Hannah looked as lovely and peaceful as she did after a long hike on her best camping days, stretched out on the sunlit sand. I asked whether I could close Hannah's eyelids, and Amy put a little Vaseline on them to help them stay shut. Toni held my hand and Joyce's while we stroked Hannah one last time. I moved behind Hannah, bent down to smell between her ears, and kissed her there, whispering "I love you, Hannah." Toni did the same. Then she gave Joyce and me warm hugs, while Amy went outside to move her van into our driveway and bring a stretcher. Hannah's body, which her cancer had often made uncomfortably warm, was beginning to cool.

Amy returned with the stretcher and covered it with a colorful purple and black blanket, one end rolled up to form a pillow. She and I slid Hannah's limp body onto the stretcher as I supported Hannah's head. Amy fluffed up the pillow, tucked Hannah's tongue back into her mouth, and moved her legs into comfortable positions. We made sure Estelle remained snugly tucked in Hannah's grasp. Then Amy covered Hannah and Estelle up to their necks with a warm indigo blanket. Hannah looked as if she had snuggled under a bedspread—*Schlupf unter die Deck* (Slip under the cover), as her lullaby had said.

Amy and I carried Hannah and Estelle through our backyard to Amy's vehicle: out the family room's French doors, where Hannah had often woofed to go outside; across the back deck where she used to lounge while I read and wrote and where, in recent weeks, she frequently lay alone; past the dune grasses Hannah had turned into her own hospice bed; through the garden gate we always padlocked to prevent her clever escapes; and into the van that would carry her away. Joyce, Toni, and I looked in on Hannah one last time. We thanked Amy again. We gave each other long hugs. After Toni left, Amy slowly backed the van that held our precious Pups. Then they were gone.

Joyce and I returned to our deserted home where Hannah Estelle, the child we have never had, had sparkled at the center of our family and friends. On this shortest day, before midnight gives way to daylight, our gracious star had left. Yet every room spoke of her presence. And we knew: Deep in the winter, amid falling snow, and all around us, we'd feel her still here. Such was our journey, a mystery without fear.

15

Spirit Traces

> Sure on this shining night
> Of starmade shadows round,
> Kindness must watch for me
> This side the ground.
>
> The late year lies down the north.
> All is healed, all is health.
> High summer holds the earth.
> Hearts all whole.
>
> Sure on this shining night I weep for wonder wandering far alone
> Of shadows on the stars.
>
> —James Agee[20]

How do you remember, deep in December, the love of a canine friend who embodied summer gold? Every day in the week after Hannah died I returned to the favorite spots she and I had visited the week before. I took my camera along, wishing to capture in images traces of her gentle spirit.

At Kruse Park, dark billowing clouds overhung the unsettled waters. I sat near the fallen tree where, one week earlier, Hannah

To Sing Once More

and I had watched a model plane glide through lake-reflected sunlight. Today a strong wind kept the clouds in constant churn. At one moment they threatened snow. At another they would part to let gossamer light-shafts stream from the mostly hidden sun. These created wide silver pools across the turbulent charcoal of Lake Michigan, like starmade shadows round. It was like seeing starlight after daybreak. It was like catching a glimpse of Hannah's spirit.

Two days later, on Christmas afternoon, I retraced our visit to Aman Park. This time I did not stay at the bench where Hannah and I had stopped a week earlier. After sitting there and taking some photographs, I walked onward to another bench, ten minutes away, where Hannah and I had often sat when we could do longer hikes. Donated by a local couple to remember two beloved dogs who liked to chase frogs there, the bench overlooks a bend in Sand Creek. Enough soil has collected in the stream to form a natural launching pad for canine water sports. When still healthy, Hannah used to glide through the water like an alligator in search of stray sticks.

Overnight a light powdering of snow had fallen, dusting the leaf-covered forest floor in delicate white. As I sat looking at the stream, the water's seamless surface mirrored every tree and branch and limb along its distant shore. To my right a partially fallen and leafless tree slanted across the creek, the snow lining its top side stenciled in its water-reflected image below. No breeze stirred. No visitors were heard. In the stillness of this beauty-stretched moment, on a midday shining night, the tree reminded me of the *Christkindleins Baum* in Hannah's *Traum*, the Christmas tree in her dream.

Many other memorial walks have followed. Nearly every weekend you can find me at one of Hannah's favorite spots, wandering far alone. When I cry, as I sometimes may, I weep for wonder, sure, on this shining night, of shadows on the stars. Yet I wish all is healed, all is health. Hannah wanders with me, our gracious star. Or, like kindness, she watches from afar. She helps this midnight walker see a great light. Because of her I learned, and still I learn, to sing once more. For her gentle spirit my gratitude overflows. High summer holds the earth. Our hearts are whole.

Epilogue: Dear Hannah

WINTER SOLSTICE, DECEMBER 21, 2018

Dear Hannah Pups,
Too soon, gone are our days.[21]

Thank you for letting us take you home with us eleven short years ago, when it must have been hard for you to leave your mom and sweet pup-mates at Cooperslane.

Thank you for trusting us to be your new (human) family, for helping us slow down, to become more attentive, more observant, and less self-absorbed.

Thank you for delivering rays of sunshine at a time when we were still grieving.

Thank you for teaching us the ways of an energetic, *joie de vivre* Canadian puppy.

Thank you for your pure, steadfast, unconditional loyalty that greeted us every single day with wagging tail and toothy smile—even on our worst days and darkest nights.

Thank you for being gentle with kitty Measha, for being considerate of brother Remy, for loving sister Sophie and all of our friends—especially Toni—and every single person you ever met, no matter who they were.

Thank you for being the best example of holy, unbiased acceptance of all people—maybe not of all dogs but certainly of all people.

Thank you for your endless tolerance and instant forgiveness and for never holding a grudge—when we accidentally stepped on your paws, pulled your collar sternly, or yanked your leash abruptly—or when we spastically yelled at you for rolling in crap, for eating thoroughly disgusting things, for swallowing socks, gloves, and plastic bags, for raiding waste baskets, devouring dirty Kleenex, sneaking cheese off the appetizer plate, and digging holes in the backyard.

Thank you for forgiving me when I called you a stinky puppy every other day.

Thank you for forgiving us when we didn't understand what you were trying to tell us, and especially for when we couldn't prevent thunderstorms and fireworks. (We promise, where you are going, there will be no thunderstorms, guns, or fireworks.)

And so, dear, dear Pups, thank you for being a steadfast, loyal companion since the day you moved into our hearts and home, especially to Lambert: for leading him to meet other people, for helping him feel less lonely and shy, for giving his days form and routine, for giving him permission to take a break.

Thank you for walking, running, and swimming with Lambert—hundreds of miles; over the rough and the smooth, amid the highs and the lows, through the light and the dark.

Thank you for making us smile and laugh every single day. If we could, we would keep you here with us forever or at least longer. If we could, we would have kept cancer from getting into your strong bones.

But too soon, gone are our days.

And now it is time, after eleven short years, to remove your leash and let you run with your old energetic, Canadian, pain-free puppy spirit over the bridge between here and a perfect unknown, where we would like to imagine you running and romping with Rosa. We miss you already. We will welcome your beautiful spirit in the shadows of this house, in the shade of the backyard and front porch, in every Golden Retriever we meet, in the mirages of our imaginations, and in our sweetest dreams. We love you, Pups.

Yours forever,

Joyce

Acknowledgments

When I first drafted this memoir during the summer of 2019, I had no clue its title would gain new poignancy one year later. The rapid spread of the coronavirus pandemic has put vocalists at heightened risk. The choirs I normally sing with have not rehearsed or performed since mid-March, nor do we expect to resume anytime soon. Like so many choristers around the world, we long "to sing once more." Perhaps my memoir helps give voice to our mutual longing.

Among the many people who have shared my vocal adventures, no one has played a larger role than Mervin Fick. A gifted singer, organist, and choral conductor, Mervin led three of the choirs I belonged to in Toronto, invited me to join him in a semi-professional men's quartet, and created many other opportunities for solo and small ensemble singing. Most importantly, he gave me empathetic and astute voice lessons for four years, with our dog Hannah always nearby. I gratefully dedicate this book to Mervin Fick, master teacher and musical friend. It is thanks to Mervin and Hannah that I learned to sing once more.

A number of friends and family members have read and responded to early versions of this book. I thank all of them for their heartfelt and supportive responses. Two in particular have drawn on their experience as writers and editors to give me insightful advice. Jean Blomquist carefully read a draft manuscript when I was still deciding whether to publish it, and she shared many encouraging comments. More recently Ronnie Shuker provided close scrutiny of the final version and made numerous helpful suggestions. Thank you, Jean and Ronnie, for your expertise, generosity, and friendship.

My journey with Hannah, from a late summer homecoming in August 2007 to her mid-winter departure in December 2018, was intimately shared with Joyce Recker, my wife. Joyce's farewell letter in this book's epilogue perfectly captures the gratitude she and I have felt for Hannah's companionship. Thank you, Joyce, for letting me include your letter and being my partner for life.

One Hannah-lover did not get to read this memoir. Ruth Recker, Joyce's mother, died just a few months after Hannah's farewell. In 2013 we had moved Mom Recker to Grand Rapids, Michigan, where she became a much-beloved resident of the Clark Retirement Community. Hannah loved Mom too. "How's my Hannah girl?" Mom would ask whenever she came to our house for a visit. Hannah would reply with soft licks and fond gazes. We brought Hannah to the Clark Retirement Community for one last visit the day before she died. A month later Mom suffered a severe episode of congestive heart failure, and she died in March 2019. I offer this book in her memory and in memory of Harold Recker, Joyce's father, who died in July 2012, one week after Joyce and I had moved back to Grand Rapids.

Although shadowed by death and unsure when to sing again, I have new dog songs in my heart. In January 2020, after I had rewritten this book, Joyce and I adopted a lovely reddish Golden Retriever named Ruby. Born in early July 2017, she was two and a half years old when I discovered her at a local adoption agency. Ruby has quickly captured our affections. Throughout all the disruption and isolation and anxiety created by the current pandemic, she has been our sweet and loyal companion. Ruby makes us laugh every day. I can only imagine how she and Hannah would have played. Yet that's what I do imagine, with a smile, as we celebrate their birthdays today.

Lambert Zuidervaart
July 7, 2020

Endnotes

1. "The People That Walked in Darkness," from the oratorio *Messiah* (1741) by Georg Friedrich Händel; the text is from Isaiah 9:2 (King James Bible).
2. Subsequently published as Lambert Zuidervaart, *Dog-Kissed Tears: Songs of Friendship, Loss, and Healing* (Eugene, OR: Wipf and Stock, Resource Publications, 2010).
3. Refrain from Loreena McKennitt, "Never-Ending Road (Amhrán Duit)," on the album *An Ancient Muse*, Quinlan Road, 2006.
4. Hannah's story reminds one of Jacob's second wife, Rachel, who gave birth at a very old age to Benjamin, her second son. (I recall Rachel's story in the first chapter of *Dog-Kissed Tears*, 3–4.) It also parallels the story of Saint Anne. According to Catholic and Eastern Orthodox traditions, Saint Anne (Hannah in Hebrew) was Jesus's grandmother. She gave birth to Mary after many years of childlessness and, when Mary was three years old, dedicated her to temple service.
5. Fifth stanza of the popular English lullaby "Twinkle, Twinkle, Little Star," originally written as a poem by Jane Taylor and first published as "The Star" (1806). Sophie learned the more familiar first stanza from Joyce; I describe the magic of this song in chapter 5 of *Dog-Kissed Tears*, 23.
6. "Turn Again to Life," words by Mary Lee Hall (1847–1918) and music by Barry Peters (2000).
7. First verse of "The Call," by the metaphysical poet George Herbert (1593–1633), as set to music by Ralph Vaughan Williams in *Five Mystical Songs* (London: Stainer & Bell, 1911), 21–22.
8. From "She's Got a Way," music and lyrics by Billy Joel, originally released on his first solo album *Cold Spring Harbor* (Family Productions, 1971) and later featured as a single from the live album *Songs in the Attic* (Family Productions, 1981), as sung in concert by The Four Men.
9. From Loreena McKennitt, "Penelope's Song," on the album *An Ancient Muse*, Quinlan Road, 2006.
10. Second stanza of William Butler Yeats, "The Lake Isle of Innisfree" (written 1888; first published 1890), as sung in concert by The Four Men, in a setting by Eleanor Daley (2002).

Endnotes

11. From Zarathustra's roundelay, as sung in the fourth movement of Gustav Mahler's Third Symphony. The German text is from Friedrich Nietzsche, *Also Sprach Zarathustra* (1883–1885), in *Friedrich Nietzsche: Werke, Kritische Gesamtausgabe*, Abt. 6, Bd. 1, edited by Giorgio Colli and Mazzino Montinari (Berlin: Walter de Gruyter, 1968). The English translation is from Friedrich Nietzsche, *Thus Spoke Zarathustra*, translated by Walter Kaufmann (New York: Penguin Books, 1966), 227–28. The voice speaking is "die tiefe Mitternacht" (deep midnight).

12. Third stanza of William Butler Yeats, "The Lake Isle of Innisfree," as sung in concert by The Four Men, in a setting by Eleanor Daley.

13. It is known as the HHHHHMM Scale, after the first letter of the main word in each criterion: *H*urt, *H*unger, *H*ydration, *H*ygiene, *H*appiness, *M*obility, and *M*ore Good Days than Bad. Each criterion can be scored from 0 (Unacceptable) to 10 (Excellent); a total score of more than 35 is deemed "acceptable quality of life for pets." The scale is adapted from Alice Villalobos, with Laurie Kaplan, *Canine and Feline Geriatric Oncology: Honoring the Human – Animal Bond* (Hoboken, NJ: Wiley-Blackwell, 2007), and it was published in the May 2008 issue of *Clinician's Brief* (Decision-Making Issues with Euthanasia, p. 23).

14. *A Quiet Place: Music for Healing III*, recorded by the Vancouver Chamber Choir, conducted by Jon Washburn, Grouse Records, 2013.

15. "Wiegenlied," music by Johannes Brahms (1868). The first verse is a traditional German folk poem modified by Clemens Brentano. The second verse, by Georg Scherer, was added later. I always sang this to Hannah in German. Here I provide my own English translation to convey its meaning more accurately than most English versions do—although with some modifications in meaning, primarily for the sake of meter and rhyme.

16. "Dido's Lament," from the opera *Dido and Aeneas* (1688) by Henry Purcell, with a libretto by Nahum Tate.

17. Third stanza from Loreena McKennitt, "Never-Ending Road (Amhrán Duit)," on the album *An Ancient Muse*, Quinlan Road, 2006.

18. Second stanza from Loreena McKennitt, "Never-Ending Road (Amhrán Duit)," on the album *An Ancient Muse*, Quinlan Road, 2006.

19. See the epilogue at the end of this book.

20. James Agee, "Sure on This Shining Night," in *Permit Me Voyage* (New Haven, CT: Yale University Press, 1934), 14; set to music by Morten Lauridsen in a well-known eponymous choral composition from his vocal cycle *Nocturnes* (2005). The text also has been set by Samuel Barber as a solo with piano accompaniment, in his collection *Four Songs* (1940), published by G. Schirmer as Barber's opus 13. Agee's text is part of a larger poem titled "Description of Elysium" (pp. 13–15) in Part I ("Lyrics") of his book.

21. "Soon gone is the day" is a line from Loreena McKennitt, "Penelope's Song," which I quote at the beginning of chapter 7. Joyce recited the lyrics to this song after reading her letter to Hannah the morning of Hannah's departure.

www.ingramcontent.com/pod-product-compliance
Lightning Source LLC
Chambersburg PA
CBHW071742040426
42446CB00012B/2440